Education and children's emotions

# Education and children's emotions:
## an introduction

Geoffrey Yarlott

Weidenfeld and Nicolson
5 Winsley Street London W1

ISBN 0 297 99374 7

Printed in Great Britain by
Willmer Brothers Limited, Birkenhead

For my mother

# Contents

# Acknowledgements

I should like to express my gratitude to colleagues and students in the School of Education at Nottingham University, and to friends in other universities and colleges of education, with whom I have enjoyed discussing the contents of this book over a number of years. It is impossible to acknowledge each individual source from which, unconsciously perhaps, one assimilates ideas, and I hope that those who have helped me to a better understanding of children's emotions will accept this expression of thanks in place of specific acknowledgement. However, I must mention my indebtedness to W. S. Harpin, who kindly read and commented on the manuscript and helped check the proofs, and to J. E. Axon, A. W. Beck, J. D. L. Hay, A. H. Stewart, and A. D. Wooster, who offered criticism and advice on sections of the book, though I must take full responsibility for what is printed here. Above all, I wish to thank the children whose experiences I have written about; they provided the original stimulus for the book.

My thanks are also due to: Blackie and Son Ltd. and the London Association for the Teaching of English, for permission to reproduce extracts from *Assessing Compositions*; to the editor, *New Society*, for the diagram of the autonomic nervous system; to Methuen and Co. Ltd. and A. Kendon, for the *Notation of facial postures*, reproduced from M. Argyle, *Social Interaction*; to Mrs William Vandivert for the photograph of S. E. Asch's social-pressure experiment; to the editor, *The Guardian*, for photographs of a girl and spectators at Wimbledon; and to The Radio Times Hulton Picture

*Acknowledgements*

Library for the photograph of a puppet-show audience.

Finally, I wish to thank: J. Shuckburgh and Miss Mary O'Connell of Weidenfeld & Nicolson Ltd., for their support and encouragement; Phyll Morris, for her patience and skill in typing the manuscript; and, as ever, my wife for her assistance at every stage of the work.

G.Y.

The University of Nottingham
*September, 1971*

# Preface

This book, which is written for teachers, student-teachers, parents, and anyone who is curious about the workings of the child's emotional life, is offered as an introduction to the subject of affective education. It is presented from an educationist's, not a psychiatrist's, standpoint, and it examines those aspects of the child's emotional experience which are amenable to educational influence. Strangely enough, while much has been written about the education of emotionally maladjusted children, very little has been written on the kind of emotional education which is appropriate for the normal child. The present book offers some suggestions to this end – suggestions which may be of interest to the science teacher as well as the arts specialist. It describes some of the procedures currently being used in our junior and secondary schools to influence children's emotions, and looks critically at the theoretical suppositions underlying these. The book also provides samples of boys' and girls' work for discussion, and offers interpretative comments upon a number of real-life situations involving children's emotions.

My aim has not been to write a treatise on emotion, but to stimulate fresh interest in the problems of emotional education. Accordingly, although I have drawn extensively on recent research findings and theoretical advances in the field of affect psychology, I have refrained from entering into elaborate technical detail. I have endeavoured to provide an explanation of emotional processes which will interest the general reader, and to suggest relevant follow-up reading for those who wish to inquire further into the subject.

Conscious of the confusion which besets the minds of

many students and teachers regarding the role of affective experiences in the educative process – their uncertainty as to their own aims and objectives, the best methods and procedures for implementing these – I have thought it advisable not to defer writing this book until such time as I could commit perfected arguments to paper, but to offer an outline of emotional education which may help the practising teacher. It is for others now to examine this suggested approach, and to decide in what ways it needs modifying or developing.

# 1 Introduction

For some time now critics have been expressing dissatisfaction with our present system of education, which, they complain, tends to emphasize the cognitive at the expense of the child's emotional development. In Holbrook's words (1961, p. 45): 'What we are forgetting and abandoning is the culture of the feelings.' The title of a recent article – 'Emotions: the missing link in education' (Beatty, 1969) – is symptomatic of this concern. There is an urge to do something positive about 'educating' emotion to offset the preponderantly intellectual emphasis in educational practice. Thus, Jeffreys (1962, p. 129) writes:

'There is as much need for the education of feeling as for the education of thinking. The one cannot be left to chance any more than the other. And, although the general emphasis in educational practice is by no means so preponderantly intellectual as it was fifty years ago, it is open to question whether we have yet appreciated all that the education of feeling involves. There is little doubt that the rather narrowly academic channel of the grammar school and the university still achieves intellectual distinction at the price of neglecting the education of feeling.'

Bantock (1967, p. 79) argues from a similar standpoint: 'We are always being told that the function of our education is to make children think.... It is equally necessary to teach children how to feel; for some such feelings are as important a way of taking the world, as apprehensive of aspects of reality, as are our cognitions.' Niblett (1963, p. 21) holds that conditions of life in our machine-dominated civilization, with its persuasive techniques of communication, are 'highly discouraging both to genuine feeling and to moral growth'. Like Jeffreys and Bantock, he suspects that 'The twentieth-century mind is happier with facts and theories than with feelings and personal commitments.'

Along with this dissatisfaction with the educational system, and with the dehumanized society it is said to reflect, there is a general concern about the deterioration of personal relationships and the incidence of violence and aggression in our civilization. Consideration and sympathy for other people's feelings, it is alleged, are becoming increasingly uncommon nowadays. The violent, anti-social behaviour of the streets is reflected in the violent material shown on cinema and television screens. Something of the public impatience with the failure of educationists to provide any remedy for these problems may be gauged from the correspondence columns of our magazines and newspapers. A correspondent, writing to the *Listener* in November 1966, expressed what many people doubtless feel:

'Sir,

'In your leader [*Listener*, November 3] you say: "Nobody really knows how far actual behaviour is affected – whether violence on the screen breeds violence in life or rather sublimates it." Then is it not high time we tried to find out? We have had some sixty years of violence on the cinema screen and thirty on television; when are the providers going to spend a few thousand pounds on research into this crucial question?'

What are teachers doing at present then regarding the education of children's emotions?

In a book entitled *The Education of the Emotions*, published as long ago as 1937, Margaret Phillips observed that 'there is often a striking contrast between the fluency with which emotional education is advocated and the vague, scanty, or tentative nature of the practical prescriptions offered to this end' (p. 14). Today, over thirty years later, this situation remains virtually unchanged. The older teacher brought up on McDougall's psychology may still regard it as his business to help children to 'refine' their raw, primitive feelings by channelling these into socially acceptable activities; other educationists, influenced perhaps by writers like D. H. Lawrence, consider it 'wrong' to interfere with a child's natural emotions and 'instincts'. Some deny that emotion can be educated, since, psychoanalysts say, a person's basic emotional characteristics are determined during infancy, before the child ever reaches the school. Others, appealing to evidence furnished by social psychology or anthropology, claim that within the limitations set by the foundational modelling of infancy, later experience is also formative. The teacher of English may seek to enlarge the pupil's sensibility, the drama specialist to provide 'release' for inhibited emotions, the art teacher to encourage the 'projection' of feeling. If there is a common denominator of emotion underlying all these different standpoints, it is not one which is readily discernible.

In the presence of so many widely differing aims and criteria the ordinary teacher is apt to be perplexed about the purposes of emotional education. Is the basic aim to control emotions, to nourish them, to refine them, or to provide therapeutic release for inhibited feelings? Or should it be to help children to achieve depth and sincerity of emotion, to develop self-awareness, and to make them more considerate for the feelings of others? Anyway, who should decide? – the teacher, the child psychiatrist, or the parent?

In this confused situation no one can be certain which teaching procedures are best for influencing the emotional make-up, or how one decides whether a person's emotions have been educated or not. Some of the procedures which might be employed, such as direct manipulation by drugs or brain surgery, or techniques like 'brain-washing' and hypnosis, we can discount, since these could not conceivably be described as 'educational'. We should need to be much clearer than we are at present moreover about our purposes in educating children's emotions before we would want to condone the sort of experimental procedure, reported in the *New Scientist* on 6 June 1968, by which Swedish children aged eleven to eighteen were shown a film, aimed at testing their emotional responses, in which 'a girl is raped by a gang of drunken youths and then forced to have sexual intercourse with a dog'. Public opinion in this country would certainly forbid the use of such methods in our schools. At the same time a more adequate rationale is needed than exists at present for many of the methods already being used – mime and movement, creative self-expression, systems of reward and punishment, and procedures like some of those recommended in the first-year Nuffield Biology Project, which, as will be shown, may produce emotional arousal where none is intended.

The causes of our uncertainty as to how to deal with children's emotions are not difficult to unravel. These will be commented upon more fully in ensuing chapters. Meanwhile it should be noted that teachers seldom receive, as part of their professional training, anything like such effective instruction on the development of children's emotions as they receive on other, related, aspects of child development – cognition, physical growth, motivation and speech. It is a striking omission, considering how much of a child's behaviour is influenced by emotion. The fact is that many of those responsible for the training of teachers are themselves not sure what emotion is. They accept its importance; they believe that emotion should somehow be educated; but they have no clear idea of where to begin.

For parents, conditioned to believe that any action they take (or do not take) is bound to affect the child's whole subsequent development, the practical problems involved in dealing with children's emotions commence from the moment of the child's birth. To feed or not to feed? The tantrums associated with bathing, weaning and toilet-training, the everyday tensions created by jealousy or sibling rivalries, involve agonies of indecision. Then come the stresses and strains associated with going to school: the problem of the child who refuses to wear a luminous road-safety jacket lest his schoolmates make fun of him; who returns home guilt-stricken because the bus conductor has overlooked his fare; who is filled with trepidation because he has been allotted a walk-on part in the school play, or been asked to sit between two girls; who, returning from what should have been an enjoyable school outing, refuses his supper and sits fretful and morose, before betaking himself to bed, where he sobs inconsolably. Later, comes the onset of puberty, with all its attendant disturbances, and the 'crisis' of adolescence, in which the challenging of parental authority and values by the young may embroil the whole family in emotional strife.

For the teacher, faced with thirty or more (other people's) children, none of whose psychic histories he knows, the problems are even more complex. His class, say, of twelve- to thirteen-year olds will have been grouped on a basis of age, intellectual ability, sex, a liking for Greek (any criterion except level of emotional development). Susan here is already three years past her menarche but several girls in the form, like the majority of the boys, are still on the younger side of puberty. The task, confronting the teacher thirty-five times a week, is to find something which interests and meets the individual needs of all these children. Unfortunately, very few things seem to interest Charlotte, who day-dreams the hours away, or Harry, whose behaviour is sometimes infantile. Peter and Simon, on the other hand, are aggressive and truculent, and their misconduct irritates other members of the class. Are these simply defence mechanisms, indicating that some basic need or physiological drive is being overlooked? The answer usually depends on whichever psychology text-book the teacher happens to consult first. Is he pitching the aspiration level too high or too low? Has he allowed enough scope for intrinsic motivation? Is it he or the parents who are at fault?

Because young children cannot, and older children cannot or often will not, verbalize their feelings adequately, the

B

teacher has to rely a good deal on intuition and his observation of pupils' facial expressions to guide him in dealing with their problems. In a few isolated cases there may be little doubt that a child is emotionally maladjusted and in need of psychiatric treatment. Grossman's book, *Teaching the Emotionally Disturbed* (1965), provides reports by American teachers on many children of this kind – 'Donald', for instance:

> 'Donald is extremely impulsive and impatient. When he knows an answer, he blurts it out because he cannot wait to be called on. If he is asked to do something he begins before he is told how do it. As soon as he has difficulty with a problem, he quits. He says whatever comes into his mind no matter how foolish or mean it is.
> Donald is extremely fearful in class. Whenever a new topic is broached he becomes convinced that he cannot master it and must be given immediate reassurance that he can. Last week he ran out of class during an examination, screaming that the work was too easy and too boring and that I did not know how to teach. He has been cutting classes recently. When he does come he is too restless to remain for the full period. Now he brings comic books to class with him in order to have something to read when he cannot concentrate. The classroom pressures are definitely too much for him.' (p. 12)

In 'Donald's' case we would not hesitate to call in expert help. Sometimes however an otherwise normal child may, under the pretext of writing an English composition, reveal a high anxiety state. Take, for example, this piece of writing done by a fat thirteen-year old girl in the 'A' form of a secondary modern school:

> 'There was a girl called Julie and she was very fat. It wasn't because she ate alot it was because she had weak glands but all the children teased her. She was very unhappy. It was Monday morning and they were having

games. The teacher told them to get into pairs but poor old Julie had not got a partner. They all called her names, and said "we dont want to be your partner your too fat to move." Julie could not stand it any longer and burst out crying. The teacher felt sorry for her and put her arm round her. At break all the children laughed at her. One day The teacher gave a race and the one that came first got a bar of chocolate. And to the teachers surprise and the childrens Julie came first now everyone was proud of her and she's never had so many friends in all her life.'

How should the teacher respond to such a fantasy? Though there are good arguments for keeping the teacher's role separate from the psychotherapist's there are some areas of teaching where it is difficult to draw the line between these.

It is comparatively rare for adolescents to project their feelings as explicitly as this, however. Often they conceal their emotions, which makes it difficult to gauge their responses accurately. I once read to a class of thirteen-year old boys a passage from Arthur Grimble's *A Pattern of Islands* describing some primitive unanaesthetized surgery and the risk of septicaemia this entailed. Suddenly, without warning, a boy at the back of the class fainted, rolling sideways from his desk and striking his head a fearful thump upon the floor. Afterwards he talked about the incident quite composedly but he could not say why he had fainted: he just found the passage unbearable. As a teacher one feels guilty when something like this happens (a reaction which itself bears looking into) – there is a sense of having violated the pupil's susceptibilities, of having let down his trust. Yet what is the conclusion to be drawn from this? That this popular third-form reader should be banned from schools? That each pupil should be psychoanalysed before being exposed to harrowing situations? In terms of the affective education of all these boys was this a wholly disastrous lesson?

Strangely enough, it is not usually the gruesome nor the

horrific which troubles boys (girls may be different), despite
the fuss that some adults make about horror comics and TV
violence. Pathos can be much more disturbing, particularly
for younger children. To a four-year old the spectacle of
Nancy Sikes' death on the screen may be less affecting than
Oliver Twist's loneliness and vulnerability. After viewing
Oliver's flight over the roof-tops and his subsequent return to
the sanctuary of Mr Brownlow's home my son, who was then
four years old, wept copiously. At the end of the film he
asked: 'Do you think he will stay with them for ever?'
Stories like *The Ugly Duckling* and Gallico's *Snow Goose*
bring tears to the eyes of many children, who seem to identify with loneliness and helplessness. A five-year old boy asked his father to read to him the adventures of Ulysses, a child's
version of which he had brought home from the children's
library. Strong stuff this for a child to go to bed on! In the
small hours of the following night the boy woke the house
with his sobbing: he was perspiring freely and obviously in
great distress. 'It's that book!' thought the father, ' – Old
Cyclops lies behind this.' Sure enough, when the boy recover-
ed sufficiently to talk about his dream it was, as the father
had suspected, *that* book. But it was not Cyclops, nor Circe,
nor the slaying of the suitors which had broken the dream
barrier. It was the pathos surrounding the death of the dog,
Argus, which proved insupportable. The point of this anecdote is that the father, who had had misgivings from the first
about reading that particular book to a child, was an
experienced teacher of English. His misgivings were justified,
but not at all for the reason he suspected.

It is extraordinarily difficult to gauge the impact which new
experiences may have upon children. It is as easy to over-
estimate this as to underestimate it. We anticipate that
youngsters will laugh at Laurel and Hardy or the clowns in
the circus, and as often as not on first exposure to these
they cry. In our pursuit of more exciting, imaginative ways
of teaching, moreover, we may unwittingly demand more of
young sensibilities than they can stand. As the handbook

on *Primary Education* (1959, p. 176) puts it: 'Teachers need to be on their guard lest they play too much on children's emotions.' This explains why some teachers have strong reservations about the degree of deliberately induced arousal which Margaret Langdon's (1961) 'intensive writing' methods entail (see p. 152 below). The exploitation of feelings like repugnance, fear and horror in what are essentially artificial, contrived situations offends against what some regard as emotional 'hygiene'. A poem of Lawrence's to Jessie Chambers (the 'Miriam' of *Sons and Lovers*) adds point to the criticism which is being implied here:

The feelings I don't have I don't have.
The feelings I don't have, I won't say I have.
The feelings you say you have, you don't have.
The feelings you would like us both to have, we neither
                                                of us have.
The feelings people ought to have, they never have.
If people say they've got feelings, you may be pretty sure
                                        they haven't got them.
So if you want either of us to feel anything at all
You'd better abandon all idea of feelings altogether.

Lawrence would have wholly endorsed Rousseau's advice on educating children: 'Be clear, direct, unemotional' (1762, p. 74)

It is not only English and the humanities which exercise pupils' emotions – a fact that is commonly overlooked. Science can exercise them too, in a far more potent sense than Newsom's coy statement (para.436) to the effect that 'emotion and science are not utter strangers' would seem to imply. The first year Nuffield Biology Project, for instance, in which investigation involves opening fertilized eggs at various stages of development to inspect the living embryo inside, sometimes produces high emotional involvement. Teachers' reactions to these aspects of the Nuffield Project produced an interesting correspondence in the *Times Educational Supplement* during April 1968.

Two writers expressed alarm at the moral implications of these experiments, suggesting that they encouraged attitudes to life and death which might have a bearing in future years upon such social problems as abortion, euthanasia and eugenics. Children experienced horror or ghoulish delight upon the realization of the inevitable death of the embryo, these writers claimed. A correspondent replied that we have to accept that plants and animals must die if school biology is to approach the study of living organisms in an inquiring way and be truly 'scientific'. The 'real' problem in school biology today, this person affirmed, is to conserve an adequate supply of animals for future experimental purposes. The emotional problem could be minimized he felt, by presenting biology in a sensible, 'especially sensitive' manner: 'If the subject is approached sympathetically children understand life-processes and do not become callous or unduly emotional about them.'

But there is an emotional problem here which, initially at least, must take precedence over moral considerations. It has less to do with callousness or ghoulishness than with the perceptual differences which individual children bring to bear upon the 'same' experiment. These can produce disturbing effects. A biologist colleague reports that the majority of a class of eleven-year old girls were deeply distressed when, in the course of one such investigation into chick development carried out recently by a student teacher, a newly hatched chick was observed to be grotesquely misshapen. Probably the egg had not been regularly turned during incubation. The chick's neck was twisted, it could not stand straight and, because the skin on one leg and on the abdomen was not complete, the muscles lay bare and the alimentary canal was visible hanging down in the peritoneum. Several girls were greatly agitated by this experience, and some could not bear to look upon the creature. There is no mistaking the emotional potency of such a lesson: it is a form of affective experience which some parents or teachers might not wish to condone. The problem is to know how to cope with the fact that no two children see the experiment in precisely the same way and that they therefore react very differently. It is not always practicable to give individual instruction, although, as the compilers of the Nuffield programme realize, each pupil has his own special needs. Perhaps the best we can do is to work with small groups, where reactions can be closely observed and group pressures minimized. Apart from that and the maintenance of all obvious precautions, biologists might also reconsider at what stage in the syllabus it is best to introduce this topic and others like it. This stage need not necessarily come later: it could come much earlier, if the experience of children born in farming communities is any-thing to go by. At least it needs to be demonstrated that the onset of puberty is the most appropriate time in an urban girl's emotional development to initiate such investigations.

So far I have concentrated mainly on this matter of predict-ing or anticipating pupils' emotional responses. The problem is sometimes to know what constitutes an emotional response. Some children, as we have seen, reveal their feelings through their behaviour; some, like 'Julie' (see pp. 6–7 above), under the thin disguise of pseudonym. Perhaps the most difficult thing of all is to gauge a child's emotionality from his written work. Let us turn finally to some writing done by two fifteen-year old boys in a London comprehensive school. Which (if either) is written under pressure of strong emotion? First, 'Howard's' essay:

### 'Saying Goodbye

Only an hour to ago befor I leves to cattes the train which will take me to portmorth with a thurnded other fellows, Going to the same place. for all your nown they mike be on the sane boat. I wounder whats its like in the R. N. Mike be good, seeing atlacing all day. And new port each week. half an hour to before the train. I wonder what mums thinkin I pett his evy her eyes out right now. Shes all. right, she won be seeing men lie every day and night. she got dads pensiver and the ransen bock. fifteen mins heft peter get redy for the startion's Come on mum where's dad, "In the car". "right." We araidy at the startions the train just aggraidy. every kissing their muns dads wives childs good bye. Well good-bye mums goodbye I write to you evert day and I see you every time I am, on leve. Bye mun, bye dad bye they must be take it bad. her only son going to war for the first time. Bye.

HOWARD'

Compare that with 'Jonathan's' essay:

'*My First Dance.*

I went to my first dance at the age of thirteen. Naturally I was nervous at the thought of meeting other people in such new surroundings, and it was not without some reluctance that I decided to go.

It was a Sunday evening, and I was at a local dance hall. I arrived there with an elder friend who had been there many times before, and he was trying to impress me a little by saying "hello" to all the girls that he knew there. There were not many people there then, for it was early. I certainly did not want to dance until the hall was more crowded, if I danced at all. For the moment, however, I just walked around with my friend, trying to be as friendly as I could with everyone he spoke to. Eventually, the place was packed out, with hardly room to move. The mixture of intense heat and thick cigarette smoke stifled me. The group was playing its music tremendously loudly, and this helped to cure me of my nervousness. Then my friend announced that he was "going to have a dance". Not wanting to be left on my own, I followed him to the dance floor.

I stood nearby, watching him dancing with what looked like a seventeen years old girl, but who was probably nearer thirteen, but wearing a great deal of make-up.

I tapped one foot in time to the rhythm of the music, but could not find anything to do with my hands. I put one in my pocket, but it sweated so much I soon had to take it out. Eventually I decided to light a cigarette, although I had never previously smoked. I lit one, and immediately felt more like the majority of the people there. Immediately after I finished it, I lit another one, because I wanted something to help me pluck up courage to dance. At the beginning of the next song, I strode out on to the dance floor and asked a girl to dance. I did not really care who the girl was. I began to dance very self-consciously, trying to make every movement of the dance look how I would have liked it to look.

We finished dancing and I felt much better mentally, but I felt unwell physically: the combination of heat, smoke, piercing noise, and actually smoking two cigarettes was beginning to take effect on me. I decided to go for a short walk in the fresh air.

I walked over to my friend to ask him if he would like to come with me, but he was in conversation with a couple of girls, so I did not interrupt him. I did not particularly want to go for a walk on my own, so who should I go with? I forgot about my illness for the moment, and went and danced with the same girl that I had danced with previously. I had planned to ask this girl to come for the walk with me immediately after that dance. The dance ended and she said the customary "thank you", and began to walk off: but I had summed up enough confidence now, and I tapped her on the shoulder and asked her if she would like to come for a walk with me.

She looked at me for a moment, and my hopes rose.

"No, thank you," she said softly, and walked away.

All the confidence that I had gathered, all my hopes came crashing to the ground. I turned around, struck dumb, my eyes watering slightly. I stumbled to the edge of the dance floor. My friend strode over to me.

'Where have you been?" he enquired, in a loud, strong voice.

"Oh, nowhere," I said in a low voice.

"Come over here, I've some girls to introduce you to," he said, waving his arm in the direction of a group of boys

and girls, all about my age. We walked over to them, and
soon I was "wrapped up" in conversation with them.
Strangely enough, the episode with that other girl had rid
me of any nervousness that I might have had, and I no
longer felt ill.

JONATHAN'

Experienced teachers and graduate students argue vigor-
ously about the 'emotionality' of these essays. The second
pin-points the flow of feeling expertly, recording Jonathan's
physical sensations and social responses precisely and, while
the climax may be a little strained, the feelings in general
seem to be well under control. *Too* controlled for some readers, who find this essay 'lacking in genuine urgency of feeling',
too 'literary and derived' to be wholly sincere. Howard uses
fewer emotive words and there is little self-conscious analysis
of his own feelings but, 'reading between the lines' some
readers say, you sense an undercurrent of 'felt' emotion. The
uncertainty and disagreement among English specialists which
discussion of these essays revealed points to the absence of
any satisfactory criteria for judging emotionality in children's
writing. It may be that such judgments are not worth attempting anyway, for reasons that will be suggested in a later
chapter.

These then are the sorts of contingency the teacher may
encounter in dealing with children's emotions. They merely
hint at the true complexities of the problem. Before grappl-
ing with these however, or considering in what sense emotion
can be 'educated', we need to identify some of the primary
sources of our present confusion.

# 2  What is emotion?

The other day I asked some graduate students training to be teachers to attempt to define an emotional response. Here is a sample of the statements they produced:

'An emotional response is a subjective, irrational response not involving logical reasoning, but based on subconscious repressed fears or desires.

Generally excitable state – more receptive state – heightened often by change in hormonal balances. Emotions may be learnt from parents, society, environment, etc. May be inborn reactions – set patterns of behaviour.

Emotion – an overwhelming sense of being held by a power which is beyond one's control: a power which though perhaps stemming from reason becomes something that reason cannot quell. Emotion is a deeply affected attitude which colours one's views towards the whole environment. It is essentially a bursting beyond rationality.

An abstract response of the mind to a subject.

Emotion: a state of mind causing adrenalin to be added to the blood stream without physical exertion. Examples: Fear, Anger, Happiness, Anxiety.

Any strong external stimulus arouses an emotional response, which is not to be confused with a response of the senses. An emotion is usually one step on from a sense response. We touch something loathsome, and we feel revulsion. We hear something beautiful and experience delight. The emotions are very easily stimulated, particularly in their baser forms, by vulgarity of any kind, be it in an artistic or a moral field.

Emotion is an intense subjective feeling induced by joy, elation, happiness, etc. or the opposite feeling of dejection, sorrow, pity, etc. There is no room for apathy, passivity or objectivity in emotion. Emotion is the ability to take part in the feelings of others or to respond to other people.'

Several of these statements touch, in an isolated way, upon important characteristics of an emotional response – glandular secretions, a heightened state of awareness, reactions to external stimuli, and so forth – but the diversity of opinion reflected in the list as a whole, the odd mixture of Platonic, psychoanalytical, physiological, moral and aesthetic elements, is revealing. It illustrates the degree of uncertainty which exists in the minds of highly intelligent people concerning the meaning of emotion.

Yet where should the educationist who wants to know more about emotion turn to for information? A good definition would provide a useful starting point. But there *is* no agreed definition of emotion, least of all among psychologists. Warren's *Dictionary of Psychology* gives eight different meanings of the term; other authorities list as many as thirteen (Masserman, 1948). Psychologists define 'emotion', in fact, according to very different theoretical standpoints. For psychoanalytical psychologists, emotion is a dynamic expression of instinct, emanating from conscious or unconscious sources. Magda Arnold (1960, vol. 1, p. 182) defines emotion as a felt tendency toward anything intuitively appraised as good (beneficial), or away from anything intuitively appraised as bad (harmful) – this attraction or aversion being accompanied by a pattern of physiological changes organized toward approach or withdrawal. Elizabeth Duffy (1941), a behavioural psychologist, denies that there is any such thing as emotion. She claims that emotion has no distinguishing characteristics, mental or physiological, which mark it off from other behavioural responses, and she suggests that we should drop the term 'emotion' altogether and cease to talk about it as though it were a separate entity. It should be replaced by a concept of 'energy mobilization and direction', as the single basic variable in behaviour, the extent of this energy release being determined by the degree of effort required by the situation as interpreted by the individual.

Although Duffy's theory is supported by D. Lindsley's work (1950, 1951) and by an impressive array of empirical evidence, psychologists have in the main been reluctant to follow her suggestion and drop the term 'emotion'. It is pointed out that intensity is only one criterion for judging emotion, and one which does not account for the very different states of mind which accompany different emotions. Ecstasy, for instance, can be just as intense as fear or anger, but we think of it as a more *agreeable* emotion. In other words, emotions differ according to the pleasure or displeasure they entail, as well as in degrees of intensity. This has led Young (1961 pp. 166ff.) to suggest that behaviour is organized on the hedonic principle of maximizing positive affectivity (delight) and of minimizing negative emotion (distress). McClelland (1955, pp. 226ff.) includes both pleasant-unpleasant and approach-avoidance dimensions in his model of affective arousal. He suggests that incoming stimuli innately arouse a state of pleasure or pain in us, with a corresponding tendency on our part to approach those stimuli which give pleasure and to avoid those which produce pain.

However, the complexities of human emotional behaviour cannot be explained in terms of simple pleasure-pain or approach-avoidance tendencies, except with considerable qualification. These primary tendencies are in fact frequently over-ruled by higher, more important, considerations. We find that human beings will often deny their immediate impulses for the sake of long-term values or goals, despite the emotional conflict this may generate. A woman, for instance, whose child is starving or in physical danger will, even at the risk of her own life or reputation, deliberately approach hazards which normally she would go to great lengths to avoid. Parents constantly set aside their own pleasures to gratify the needs and desires of their children. Similarly, a powerful social motive, like the desire to enhance self-esteem or win approval in the eyes of the peer group, exerts pressure upon children which sometimes causes them to disregard their more immediate impulses. Thus a child can be egged on by his friends to do something mischievous or dangerous which, but for this social pressure, he would not dream of undertaking. In such cases the conflict between self-preservation and a stronger motivation which over-rules the primary biological tendency often gives rise to emotion.

The psychoanalytical hypothesis, as presented in the writings of Melanie Klein, Joan Riviere, Anna Freud, Ian Suttie and Susan Isaacs – writers who have had a considerable impact upon English educationists – approaches emotion from quite a different standpoint. It asserts that the child's mind is a maelstrom of primitive fantasy, swept by overpowering impulses of love, hate, destructiveness, fear, guilt and jealousy, all mainly sexual in character, which are *there* in the child's mind before knowledge and understanding develop, and which constantly pull the child in different directions. As a theoretical interpretation of phenomena which admittedly are difficult to explain, this hypothesis is a fascinating one. Unfortunately, the concepts it employs are largely unverifiable and it is not a theory which enables one to predict a child's emotional behaviour very accurately. For behavioural psychologists, this notion of an inner life that is inaccessible to direct observation is a speculative red herring which merely renders the problem of understanding emotion more insoluble.

Apart from this problem of reconciling different psychological theories, a further difficulty in defining 'emotion' derives from the fact that words commonly used to signify emotion enjoy so loose a currency in everyday language. The English verb 'to feel', for example, can be used to express emotion (I feel frightened), sensation (I feel a pain in my toe), motive (I feel like kissing her), sentiment (I feel a love for my country), inner physiological state (I feel sick), vague apprehension (I feel something is about to happen), perception (I feel the bristles upon my chin), even cognition (I feel there

is something wrong with this argument) (Ryle, 1949, p. 103).
The etymological sources of this confusion are deep-rooted.
According to the OED, 'emotion' derives from the Latin
*emovere*, meaning 'to move away or agitate', while 'feeling'
derives from the Anglo-Saxon *felan* – 'to explore by touch'.
But 'motive' too derives from a word pertaining to movement (*motivus*) while 'sentiment' and 'sensation' both derive
from *sentire*, meaning to perceive or feel. In the past these
meanings were probably never very clearly differentiated and,
since any of them can now be expressed through the single
verb 'to feel', some confusion among terms like 'emotion',
'motive', 'feeling' and 'sensation' is almost inevitable. It is
because of this inherent imprecision in everyday words
relating to emotion that psychologists are driven to seek
alternatives for them. Some of the terms used in everyday
speech to signify emotion – grief, pity, ecstasy, remorse,
nostalgia, pathos – rarely occur in psychological accounts of
'affect' or 'orexis'. In such a confused situation it is small
wonder that the educationist, like Humpty Dumpty, is tempted to make the term 'emotion' mean whatever he chooses
to make it mean.

Another cause of uncertainty is the fact that no reliable
study of emotional development from infancy to adulthood
has yet been accomplished. We know a good deal about
emotional development in infancy, much less about the subsequent stages by which children progress to maturity. The
Plowden Report pin-points the inadequacy of our present
knowledge in this matter:

'We know a little about what happens to the child who is
deprived of the stimuli of pictures, books and spoken
words; we know much less about what happens to a child
who is exposed to stimuli which are perceptually, intel-
lectually or emotionally inappropriate to his age, his state
of development, or the sort of individual he is. We are
still far from knowing how best to identify in an individual
child the first flicker of a new intellectual or emotional

awareness, the first readiness to embrace new sets of concepts or to enter into new relations' [para. 9].

As Plowden explains, we need to know more about the precise relationship between biological and environmental factors in the pattern of emotional development. Is there a development from a general state of emotionality to an increased differentiation of feeling? Are there laws governing the interplay of different emotions? At what age do children learn to identify their own feelings?

Reliable longitudinal studies might throw light on the formation of underlying dispositions and persistent fears and anxieties in children. They could show how in the course of normal development some fears gradually wane while others develop, and they might suggest means by which, if it were considered desirable, these processes could be accelerated, retarded, or otherwise manipulated. Unfortunately, longitudinal studies of this sort are difficult to come by. Ideally, we need a record extending from birth (or even conception) to twenty-one years and beyond, an undertaking which would present formidable practical problems. There is also the likelihood that the very concept of emotion would change during this period of time. One has only to compare the Spens Report's (1938, pp. 133-40) account of emotional development with Plowden's (1967, paras. 65-74) to realize how much the 'official' standpoint on this matter has altered over the past thirty years, as (in this case) the impact of social psychology has undermined the prestige of McDougall's earlier instinctual theory, upon which Spens' description of emotion was largely based.

While the concept of emotion remains so ill-defined, any hypotheses we frame must be tentative. Take the questions proposed above as possible starting-points: 'Are there laws governing the interplay of different emotions?' 'At what age do children learn to identify their own feelings?' Both questions, which are of special interest to teachers, pre-suppose that there are feelings (plural), whereas some psychologists argue that only feeling (singular) exists, as a variable one-dimensional, energy level. I am not concerned here to evaluate the one-dimensional theory: the fact that it exists demonstrates the difficulty of devising a developmental study the theoretical basis of which would be acceptable to every specialist in this field.

Magda Arnold's *The Nature of Emotion* (1968), a recent symposium, illustrates some of the major divergencies of theoretical standpoint which exist at present in regard to the concept of emotion. There is still no general agreement among psychologists as to whether, for example, it is a function of emotion to organize or disorganize behaviour. The eminent American psychologist, R. S. Woodworth (1940), holds that emotion is something we learn gradually to live without as we develop better resources for coping with life's situations. As we mature, he writes, 'the practical life of relation dominates more and more over the emotional life, so that the child's behaviour becomes less emotional as he grows older' (p. 432). 'If all behaviour were well organized and directed towards a goal', declares P. T. Young (1961, p. 344), 'there would be no need for a concept of emotion.' These statements imply that emotion is essentially disruptive, something the well-adjusted adult can manage to live without.

Psychologists like R. W. Leeper and M. Arnold object to the idea that emotion is something to outgrow. Leeper (1948, 1970), while conceding that extreme emotion is disruptive, argues that, in general, emotional processes organize behaviour, since they arouse, sustain, and direct activity. Arnold (1960, vol. 1, p. 132) points out that the tender emotion a mother feels toward her child does *not* diminish, and that the disorganization or 'conflict' theorists fail to account adequately for 'positive' emotions like love, affection, and delight. According to Arnold, emotions are action tendencies: they prompt us to contend for 'possession' of those objects which we cherish, and to seek to prolong this possession whenever we achieve it. Both 'conflict' and 'organization'

c

theories thus locate emotion within a context of action, holding that emotion is occasioned by either the frustration or the facilitation of behaviour. Peters (1962) points out that emotions also arise out of wish-fulfilment, where no actual action is necessarily undertaken. A person may wish that the circumstances in which he finds himself were otherwise, yet take no positive steps to alter these circumstances.

It is perhaps worth mentioning at this point, although I do not wish to pursue the topic at present, that the disagreement between 'conflict' and 'organizational' theorists is probably less fundamental than might be supposed. Some of the main issues involved appear to have as much to do with semantics as psychology. The major 'organizational' theorists (Cannon, Leeper, Arnold) all accept in fact that emotion is occasionally disruptive, just as the leading 'conflict' theorists (Woodworth, Young, Hebb) all acknowledge that some affective processes facilitate behaviour. Unfortunately, each writer employs a different terminology for distinguishing these processes, and much of the controversy stems from this fact. For example, Leeper (1948) and Arnold (1960, vol. I, pp. 157-8) criticize Young for restricting the use of the term 'emotion' to affective disturbance. Young (1961, p. 356 would rather substitute terms like 'feeling', 'sentiment', 'interest' and 'mood' for those forms of affective process which '*are* facilitative and organizing rather than disrupting'. Leeper and Arnold, on the other hand, insist that it is emotion which is facilitative, and they complicate the matter further by equating emotion with 'motive' or 'felt action tendency'. And yet, what all three writers have to say about the organizing qualities of an affective process like 'sentiment' is remarkably similar. The real point at issue, it seems, is to decide what terminology should be employed to distinguish between emotional disturbance and those processes (also called emotional) which are inherently organizing and motivating (Hebb, 1949, p. 237).

Another problem, encountered by educationist and psychologist alike, is that it is not always easy to identify or measure emotion with any great certainty. Most of the instruments which are used for detecting emotion (as will be shown in Chapter 6) are limited or deficient in one respect or another. Close observation of another person's facial expression, bodily posture and vocal tone provides useful information about his emotional state, provided we know that person sufficiently well and are witnesses to the situation in which these non-verbal responses are elicited. But sometimes it seems as though there is 'no art to find the mind's construction in the face'. That is why it is so difficult to say just what emotion the face of the girl in plate 1 is registering. Or consider the faces of strangers on a fairground roundabout. Individual faces register dismay, anxiety, terror, delight, and yet apparently these people are all undergoing an identical experience. Asked to describe their experiences on the roundabout individuals might report a sinking feeling in the pit of the stomach, a melting sensation in the limbs, light-headedness, goose-pimples or a dryness in the throat — symptoms indicating that their emotions were accompanied by certain bodily changes. But unless he chose to describe it for us we could have little idea what any individual's mental state was, while most of the physiological changes he experienced would be hidden from our eyes (Martin, 1965).

How the bodily and the mental components of emotion are related is something no one has yet succeeded in explaining. The difference between a twinge of rheumatism and a twinge of remorse is easily recognised, but what is the connection between physical manifestations of fear (shivers down the spine and hair standing on end) and our subjective awareness of fear? How does subjective emotion enter into our nervous, electro-chemical processes? At what point does neurophysiological statement become subjective fear? It has been suggested that this relationship is not one of cause and effect: that the physical and the psychical belong rather to two different systems which contain *equivalent* statements of the same phenomena, although in different 'logical languages'. This idea of parallel systems is rejected by Suzanne Langer

(1967, p. 21), who argues that the physical and the psychical are phases of a single process rather than logically different entities. It is rather like heating a poker: at a certain point in the process a glowing redness (subjective awareness) gradually appears.

In the face of so many conflicting viewpoints and uncertainties it would appear that psychological and philosophical analyses of emotion pose almost as many problems as they solve. How is it possible to reconcile all these different explanations? And if they cannot be reconciled which, if any of them, should we adopt? The truth is that no one theory accounts adequately for all the complexities of human emotional behaviour (any more than the present book can lay claim to) although several provide valuable insights into particular aspects of it. The problem is to find some way of combining all these insights into a coherent and intelligible pattern. This is possible, I believe, only if we conceive of human nature as operating broadly according to two fundamentally opposing tendencies, each of which acts reciprocally as a balancing control upon the other. On the one hand, there are conservative elements in our make-up, which encourage dependency, avoidance of risks, and preference for security and relaxation of tension; on the other hand, there is an outgoing, exploratory urge which seeks greater autonomy, preferring thrills, adventure, novelty and stimulation to ease and comfort. Our emotions are determined according to whichever of these basic tendencies happens to be dominant at any given time. When we run away from, submit to, or appeal for help in a critical situation, the emotions we feel are different from those we experience if we face up to and triumph over a situation unaided.

Classical theories of motivation all tend to explain behaviour as a sort of balancing out of two opposite tendencies, these opposites being variously described as tension and relaxation, approach and avoidance, pleasure and pain. According to neurophysiologists, all our physical manifestations of emotion – blushing, crying, goose pimples, shivers down the spine, secretion of adrenalin, and the like – can be explained in terms of variations in the nerve impulses flowing through the sympathetic and parasympathetic divisions of the autonomic nervous system, two divisions which operate in harness as a sort of dual antagonism. The sympathetic nervous system is responsible for enabling us to adapt to sudden changes in our environment and for fitting us for those real-life emergencies in which we are prone to experience emotions like fear, anger, excitement and aggression. During sympathetic innervation, which is set in motion after the sense receptors have given warning of an impending emergency, the digestive processes are slowed down and the blood flow is shunted from the digestive system to the brain and muscles where it is more urgently needed. The heart beats more rapidly, breathing quickens, the liver releases sugar for energy, hair is erected and there may be an increase in sweating. A fourth form grammar school boy provides a light-hearted description of the sort of feelings a person experiences during sympathetic innervation.

*The Passion Of Two Biologists*
Darling!
Our genes determined that we should love each other
For the ventricles of my heart pulsate when you are in the vicinity.
The fluid of life flows round my body and
Increases to one hundred and four, centigrade.
My capillaries dilate,
Forcing the blood to my stratified epithelium, and
Causing a pale pink colouration on my face.
My sensory perceptors stimulate my brain via my axons,
Thus increasing my awareness of your presence.
The mid-joints of my lower limbs gelatinize,
And the pituitary gland at the base of my brain
Stimulates the adrenalin,
Pumping into my stomach.

This description, while not strictly accurate, will suffice for

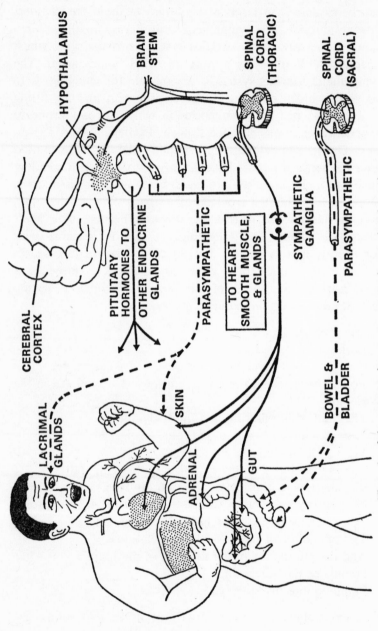

The role of the autonomic nervous system in emotional reactions

purposes of illustration within the context of the present discussion.

As Cannon (1932) pointed out, the general discharge of energy in sympathetic innervation can be harmful unless it is transformed into immediate action. If no action ensues, then the bodily changes associated with this 'flight-fight' reaction (as it is called) can in themselves be profoundly upsetting. This accounts for the choked, pent-up feeling we experience when a sympathetically aroused emotion like anger is prevented from finding free outlet. Fortunately, the body has its own built-in mechanisms for preserving and maintaining internal equilibrium. Whenever there is excessive sympathetic arousal, the counter-balancing effects of the parasympathetic nervous system soon begin to operate in an opposite direction, slowing down and checking sympathetic activity and preventing further action. There is secretion of acetylcholine, whose effects are nearly opposite to those of adrenalin and nor-adrenalin, which the sympathetic system secretes. Breathing and heart rate are slowed down and the digestive activity which was temporarily suspended is restored. This stabilizing tendency is regulated partly by homeostatic mechanisms and to some extent by voluntary behaviour. Rather than be constantly remedying an internal imbalance we take care to avoid conditions which are potentially dangerous or which would generate emotion unnecessarily. We avoid bright lights, extremes of temperature, loud sounds, electric shocks and other stress-inducing stimuli. Our biological survival partly depends upon the taking of such obvious precautions.

Psychoanalytical and drive theories likewise explain motivated behaviour as a gravitation towards equilibrium and the relaxation of emotional tension. According to Freud (1948):

'In the psychoanalytical theory of the mind we take it for granted that the course of mental processes is automatically regulated by the pleasure principle: that is to say, we believe that any given process originates in an unpleasant

state of tension and thereupon determines for itself such
a path that its ultimate issue coincides with the relaxation
of this tension, i.e. with avoidance of pain or with produc-
tion of pleasure. . . .' (p. 1)

Freud's account of motivation rests on the hypothesis that
'there is an attempt on the part of the psychic apparatus to
keep the quantity of excitation present as low as possible, or
at least constant'. The basic premise of Hull's drive theory
is somewhat similar. Hull (1951) assumes that behaviour is
motivated by energies such as sex, hunger and thirst, arising
out of homeostatic imbalance or tension. For example, when
we are hungry a tension is set up which activates a hunger
drive, and this directs behaviour to the acquisition of food.
Once we have eaten, the tension is reduced and equilibrium
is restored. Approach-avoidance theories likewise regard
motivation as a sort of balancing out of pleasurable and
painful tensions, claiming that we tend to approach stimuli
known to arouse pleasure, and to avoid those known to
produce pain.

   Now it is true, as we all know from observation, that
human beings – older people especially – do tend to avoid
strain and excessive stimulation. People prefer to live for
much of their lives in a relaxed, low-keyed relationship with
their environment, rather like the mariners in Tennyson's
*The Lotos-Eaters*. This general law in human nature is reflected in a corresponding tendency in other animal species.
At its most primary, biological level, in fact, our emotional
life has a good deal in common with that of other creatures.
(It is also much more complex for, though I do behave like
an animal sometimes, I at least know when I am doing so.)
There is something of the cat enjoying the comfort of the
fireside in all of us. In such cosy circumstances our demeanour
is generally friendly and benign, and we experience a sense
of secure well-being. Scores of our favourite popular songs,
like *Home Sweet Home*, Ivor Novello's *We'll Gather
Lilacs* or a record of John McCormack singing *The Old*

*House,* express this pleasurable sense for us, or nostalgic yearning for it. It is restful and emotionally satisfying, even for children, to withdraw occasionally from the world and, with the aid perhaps of music, books, or the quiet of the countryside, retreat from life's stresses and tensions. A poem by a thirteen-year old girl expresses the sort of emotional attachment which everyone has felt at some time or another for those half-remembered, half-imagined, golden days when life seemed so much cosier and more placid than at present.

We collected eggs from the farm down the road
The clock tower house
And the lady who lives there –
The people all walked together on Sundays
The flower borders were neat
The lawns cut and trimmed.
The old men in white hats
Rolled bowls on the green
Their wives sitting chatting –
Not watching the game.
I was up in the attic with my box of toys
Or down by the river
Catching tiddlers in nets.
Town streets, when we go shopping,
Are always so crowded;
The shops full of people eager to chat.
There is so much noise and bustle
At market on Monday –
Happy were the days when I stayed with my Gran.

Experienced, professional writers like, say, Betjeman, Patience Strong or H. E. Bates, express the same feeling more vividly and with greater sophistication.

Yet no healthy person wishes to insulate himself permanently from bustle and noise, nor to eliminate physical risk and danger entirely from his life. Even the cat tires of the fireside eventually and begins to evince curiosity about the beckoning world outside, and so it is with human beings.

It is a paradox of our nature that after protracted avoidance of stimulation and emotional tension we begin actually to crave for these. Whether we choose to call this urge an 'aggressive instinct' or innate disposition, as some ethologists do, or an 'intrinsic motive' toward gaining greater interaction with the environment (White 1959), does not greatly matter. Either way, these are perhaps only alternative labels for the same outgoing tendency. Psychologists are right to emphasize that in the long run there is a gravitation toward constant equilibrium, but it needs emphasizing equally that, far from always avoiding tension and excitement, animals and human beings frequently go out of their way to welcome these. Rats which have had electrodes implanted in the 'pleasure centres' of their brains will stimulate themselves by the hour for the pleasure such self-stimulation apparently gives them (Olds, 1956). Human beings find Nirvana and the life of the lotos-eater intolerable after a time: they eventually become irritable and bored if deprived of stimulation and activity.

A graphic illustration of the human desire for novelty and stimulation is provided by some experiments on the effects of sensory deprivation conducted by Heron (1954) and his collaborators at McGill University (reported in the *Scientific American*, January 1957):

> 'The subjects were male college students, paid $20 a day to participate. They lay on a comfortable bed in a lighted cubicle 24 hours a day for as long as they cared to stay, with time out only for meals (which they usually ate sitting on the edge of the bed) and going to the toilet. They wore translucent plastic visors which transmitted diffuse light but prevented pattern vision. Cotton gloves and cardboard cuffs extending beyond the fingertips restricted perception by touch. Their auditory perception was limited by a U-shaped foam rubber pillow on which their heads lay and by a continuous hum of air-conditioning equipment which masked small sounds.'

All the subjects found this sensory isolation quite intolerable.

They wanted stimulation so badly that they would ask to hear a recording of an old stock market report played over and over. After a time they suffered loss of concentration, became confused, irritable or showed childish emotional responses. Finally they began having visual hallucinations. Although they were asked to stay for as long as possible, most subjects could stand only two or three days of it. This experiment, artificial though it is, points to the strength of the human desire for stimulation and interaction with the environment, and to the emotional repercussions of being deprived of such stimulation. The normal functioning of the brain appears to depend on a continuing arousal reaction and constant sensory bombardment.

We are now beginning to appreciate that at certain stages in their development children need stimulation and the excitement of physical danger just as much as at other times they need security and protection – a fact which is borne out by the number of games they play which are a direct response to the seduction of danger and adventure (Opies, 1969). 'Last across the road' and, among older adolescents, the 'ton-up' cult are obvious manifestations of this need for emotional excitement. Or consider this passage by a fourteen-year old girl, describing the exhilaration she experiences while living dangerously on a motor-scooter pillion:

'... We overtake the scooter in front, we are overtaking the next, and the next. We are in front. I can feel the wind rushing in my face. My head is throbbing. Faster and faster we go. The wind has blown all my hair back. My eyes are watering. The blood is poundng in my head. My eyes are streaming. My ears are getting cold. I put my head down and the wind rushes over my head. A scooter has come up and overtaken us. We go faster and come up beside it, we are side by side, we are in front. I feel exhilerated, I feel like shouting, I feel happy' (Holbrook, 1967, p. 42).

Clearly, there is an emotional thrill to be had from flirting with danger which satisfies some deep urge in our nature.

It is this urge, presumably, which accounts for the popularity of the big dipper and other hair-raising experiences which the modern fairground supplies. It helps to explain perhaps why people will pay money to see Dracula and Frankenstein films, which they know in advance will be terrifying, and why children insist on watching television programmes like *Dr Who*, although half beside themselves with fear while actually doing so.

This paradox in our nature – the need for tension-reduction and relaxation on the one hand, and for increase of tension and stimulation on the other – is partly dictated by the requirements of our biological tissues. Periods of rest are needed for restoration and growth, but occasional tension and arousal are also indispensable because of the tonic effects these have upon the body's adaptive mechanisms. As Rycroft (1968) explains, our cell tissues and organs probably benefit from a regular exercise of all the functions of which they are capable, including responses to emotional stress and anxiety. In the sheltered conditions of modern urban living there is a likelihood that some youngsters may be deprived of the natural opportunities for excitement and thrills which, biologically, they need. In this respect they may be less fortunate than their parents.

It is necessary of course to protect children from some of the various artificial hazards which civilized life puts in their way – electrical and gas appliances, patent medicines, chemical detergents, pesticides and weed-killers – but we should not be overprotective and guard them too carefully in situations where it is not necessary. It is interesting to find, for example, that doctors at the Peckham Health Centre discovered that quite tiny children could be safely left in the sloping shallow end of a swimming bath. Provided no adult interfered with them, they would teach themselves to swim, exploring the water gradually and never venturing beyond the point at which they began to feel unsafe. Similarly, children would teach themselves to ride bicycles and use gymnasium equipment, and did so more confidently and quickly than if adults tried either to urge them on or warn them to be careful (Storr, 1968, p. 42). There is an innate tendency in every child urging him to master difficulties and dangers, and an emotional satisfaction to be gained from successfully overcoming new challenges. Children may themselves be the best judges of what degree of tension and stress is tolerable to them in facing up to these challenges. Left to themselves, they will go only so far in the pursuit of dangerous activities, whereas, if an adult obstructs their urge to experiment, they may round on him with feelings of anger or frustration. We can cater for this outgoing tendency to some extent by providing facilities and opportunities which allow it free scope within a relatively 'safe' context – adventure playgrounds, gymnasia, sports centres, Duke of Edinburgh award schemes, the Youth Hostelling Association, the Outward Bound Movement and the Voluntary Service Organization. R. F. Mackenzie's book, *Escape from the Classroom* (1965), contains some unconventional hints as to how it can also be catered for in the course of a child's general education. Of one thing we can be certain: if children are not given opportunities for risking their necks and doing dangerous things occasionally just for the fun of it, they will inevitably devise their own ways of satisfying this urge to experience emotional 'kicks'. Doubtless, many of the cases which come before juvenile courts are symptomatic not so much of delinquent or criminal tendencies, as of the need to manufacture excitements and thrills in an environment which on the whole largely denies these.

# 3 The roots of emotion

Instead of pressing for a precise definition of 'emotion' it may be more useful at this stage to consider some of the basic characteristics of an emotional response. One of the first things to notice about emotion is that it invariably relates to some particular situation or some specific object (if we take the word 'object' in its widest sense to include not only concrete physical things, but other people, wants, ideas, values, standards of behaviour, social conventions – anything which a person might see as being peculiarly important to himself). Thus, in talking about emotion, we say 'I am happy when. . .', 'It makes me angry if . . .', 'What upsets me is . . .', 'I am sad because . . .'. Similarly, we feel angry *at* something, frightened *of* something, guilty or pleased *about* something. Emotion is never vague nor objectless therefore: it arises because a person appraises some situation or object as affecting himself. Even the seemingly vague sense of dread or depression which everyone experiences at one time or another can usually be traced back to some particular circumstance, if one examines the matter closely enough (Kenny, 1963, p. 60). The objects which elicit emotion are not limited of course to the present moment nor the actual environmental situation in which a person finds himself. Thoughts of past situations or of what is going to happen in the future can also arouse emotion, as can the vicarious situations which we encounter and identify with in reading books or watching films.

An object which has once aroused emotion in us does not necessarily arouse emotion each time we encounter it, and it may arouse different emotions on different occasions. A commonplace object like a motor car, for instance, normally arouses scarcely a flicker of interest, and yet it is not difficult to imagine situations in which it might induce strong emotions. For example, a would-be purchaser looks at a car with feelings of envy or keen anticipation; as he tests it on a motorway he may experience a kind of euphoria; he shows it off with pride; but, later, he may view the car with resentment or anger because it has not lived up to the quality claimed for it by the salesman; it alarms and frightens him if it behaves badly on corners; he wishes he had never bought the car if it results in injury to himself or one of his family. In all these instances attention tends to focus upon the car as the most obvious, tangible element in the situation but, although the car is the object of the emotion, it is the man's motives in purchasing and using the car which supply the emotional energy. Emotion occurs, in short, whenever we interpret a situation or object as bearing favourably or unfavourably upon the attainment of our goals, the degree and intensity of the emotion being roughly proportional to the strength of the motivation involved.

What motivates a man to buy a car? He buys it perhaps because quite simply he wants to own it or, although he may not openly admit it, because he wants to show it off to his friends. He enjoys the sense of freedom and independence which motoring gives him; he likes being able to get to and from work more quickly; he enjoys taking the family out on Sundays. While he is actually driving the car, other motivations come into play: he drives quickly to keep pressing appointments; he drives slowly and carefully for reasons of economy, or to avoid the danger of collision; he sometimes drives recklessly just to prove that he is as fast as the next man on the road. All these are examples of motivated behaviour, explaining why he acts as he does.

Apart from certain involuntary or purely reflex actions (like blinking or the jerking of one's leg if the knee is struck lightly with a rubber hammer) all behaviour is motivated, whereas not all behaviour is emotional. What determines whether behaviour becomes emotional depends upon both the *how* and the *why* of behaviour. Has a person the requisite knowledge or skill for carrying out the pattern of actions necessary for achieving his goal? Dressing in the morning, choosing a breakfast cereal, cycling to school, selecting a book from the library and studying it, entering into a class discussion – all these are examples of motivated behaviour, and normally they entail little or no emotion. Provided these actions involve accustomed patterns of behaviour, which a child can perform more or less expertly, he is able to take them in his stride. If, however, any of them demands a strange, unfamiliar pattern of behaviour, or if the execution of one of them is unexpectedly thwarted by some insuperable obstacle, then, depending on the strength of the motivational urge, emotion is likely to be generated.

Thus, it is motivation – the why of behaviour – which initiates and sustains actions, determining why we choose to to do this rather than that, how long we persevere with it, and whether we drop the action when something else engages our attention. And it is the *how* of behaviour – our repertoire of knowledge, skills and adaptive resources – which determines our capacity for achieving our goals. Both aspects of behaviour have a bearing upon emotion, as a simple illustration will demonstrate.

If a child is accustomed to riding a bicycle on the public highway, then cycling to school is a pattern of behaviour which he can presumably execute with some expertise. So long as nothing untoward develops to overtax his capabilities, then he is unlikely to experience any emotion other perhaps than mild pleasure in the sensation of motion or slight annoyance because it is raining and there is a head wind to contend with. But suppose a development occurs which catches him unprepared and without adequate resources for dealing with it. His bicycle chain suddenly slips off and becomes tightly jammed, so that his progress toward school is abruptly arrested. If he is unable to free the chain and there is no one available to assist him, what happens next will be determined largely by the strength of his desire to get to school. The motivation may simply weaken and the goal be abandoned altogether, or a determination may be aroused in him to get to school somehow even if he has to walk there. Depending on other factors which influence the situation (the time available to get to school, the importance of what is likely to happen there, how he imagines his parents' or the teacher's reactions) there may be tears and despondency, or he may kick the offending machine in impotent rage and frustration. Whatever form it takes, the child's emotional reaction will depend upon the strength of his motivation, upon his appraisal of the situation, and upon the particular resources he possesses for dealing with it.

The energy needed to initiate and sustain motivated behaviour, and to enable us to deal with problems set by the environment, rises and falls constantly along a continuum of activation – a fact which can be readily demonstrated (Lindsley, 1950, 1951). Changes in respiration, pulse rate and biochemical secretion are going on all the time, in fact, whether we are awake or asleep, and whether we are feeling emotion or not. Looked at purely from a physiological angle indeed, it is difficult to distinguish emotional reactions from the processes of normal activation, except to notice that they tend to occur at the extremes of the continuum of activation, where the mobilization of energy either reaches a climax (as during excitement) or falls to a level well below normal (as when a person is depressed). This explains why physiological reactions are often observed to increase some minutes before a person actually feels any emotion, and why the effects of an emotion like anger take so long to subside. The subjective experience of anger can be quite short lived, whereas the hormones released into the bloodstream during the emotional reaction may have prepared the body for a prolonged period of exertion.

The energy which increased motivation provides both sustains behaviour and, up to a certain point, it also improves the quality of performance. (Hence, educational text-books are constanly reminding us that it is the highly motivated pupil

D

who performs best and learns most quickly and effectively.) But if motivation is too strong it may produce a surplus of energy and, unless this energy is quickly expended, the person soon begins to show signs of emotional strain. A child waiting to go on stage at a school concert, for example, feels butterflies in his tummy and his palms feel clammy and moist. These mild signs of perturbation will not necessarily impair his performance, and they will normally disappear quickly once he goes on stage and starts to make use of the energy which has been building up inside him. This keyed-up feeling of suppressed tension and excitement is not necessarily unpleasant in fact, provided that there is not too much at stake. It partly accounts for the attraction of children's games like 'Hide and Seek' and 'What's the time, Mr Wolf?', where much of the fun consists in containing one's emotional excitement while waiting to be detected or chased.

But if we are motivated too strongly in proportion to our potential to face up to a situation, then the situation is likely to become too intense for us, in which case we may become confused and slightly disorganized. There may be lapses of memory, stammering, blushing, tears, or even fainting – all signs of emotion due to excessive motivation. When a goal is blocked by some physical, social or even imaginary obstacle, frustration (which can easily turn into aggression or anger) commonly results. Or there may be excess motivation simply because some other person is watching us. We want to perform well but, because our behaviour is being subjected to scrutiny, we become 'all fingers and thumbs', and we fumble confusedly over things which we could normally 'do with our eyes shut'. This is particularly true of the nervous pupil in school for, as Holt (1964) puts it:

'A teacher in class is like a man in the woods at night with a powerful flashlight in his hand. Wherever he turns his light, the creatures on whom it shines are aware of it, and do not behave as they do in the dark. Thus the mere act of his watching their behaviour changes it into something very different. Shine where he will, he can never know very much of the night life in the woods' (p. 21).

Excess motivation may likewise occur if the desire to do something is inhibited by some powerful moral or social constraint, or when we are faced simultaneously with two incompatible incitements to act, and cannot decide which course of action to take (Fraisse, 1968, p. 133).

The kinds of motive capable of energizing human behaviour are of course many and varied. Adults are motivated, for example, by their physiological need of food, water and oxygen; by the intrinsic urge to explore and gain greater competence in mastering the environment; by extrinsic rewards (money, material possessions, status and power); by sexual urges; by social motivations (the desire for self-actualization, love and belonging); by rational objectives and deliberate decisions to carry through long-term projects and plans; by ideological goals, political loyalties, cultural objectives, and the like. Any one of these motivations may give rise to emotion in situations where the attainment of the desired goal is seen to be hazardous or uncertain. It is a complex matter, however, to analyse adult emotions, since grown-ups differ widely both in the nature of their motives and in their individual capacities for realizing their goals. It is an easier task to examine how emotions originate in infancy, where motives are simpler and there are fewer variables to complicate the issue.

During infancy, feelings are expressed more nakedly and unselfconsciously than at any subsequent period in our lives and, although the infant's range of emotion is narrower than the adult's, the fact that he expresses his feelings so intensely enables us to study them fairly objectively. Strictly speaking, of course, we can never be sure what an infant is consciously feeling because he cannot express his feelings in words, and we can only make inferences about what he experiences. On the other hand, a tiny baby has internalized none of the social restraints and inhibitions which cause adults to repress or conceal their emotions. He knows nothing of sentiments, of moral or aesthetic emotions, of what it is to feel consideration for other people's feelings or seek emotional thrills just for the fun of it. He has assimilated none of the values and attitudes which will shape his later emotional behaviour; he cries or goes red in the face without thought that he may be letting down his self-image in public. Indeed, he has no such self-image.

The earliest human responses appear to be simply responses to biological tensions – caused by bodily discomfort, pain and hunger (although in contrast to this view, writers like Melanie Klein and Susan Isaacs claim that even babies are capable of experiencing emotions like anxiety, fear, distress, rage and love – a claim which, unfortunately, is difficult to substantiate). When a baby is uncomfortable, he cries, kicks jerkily, moves restlessly about or turns red in the face; when he is comfortable, warm and satiated, he sleeps or lies still. According to K. Bridges (1932), the baby's first affective response is a vague general excitement, which can be produced by a variety of stimulating conditions. He becomes aroused when a bright light shines in his eyes, at being suddenly picked up, put down or restrained, at the approach or withdrawal of the nipple, or at any sudden noise. His arm and hand muscles tense, his breathing quickens, his eye-lids arch and his legs kick spasmodically. At this stage his responses to pleasurable and unpleasurable stimuli are not clearly differentiated. There is simply a diffuse, total response involving the whole body and nervous system. This general capacity to respond to a variety of stimulating conditions has obvious survival value: it is the infant's way of informing the world of his needs, and of enlisting aid to correct situations which call for attention. At first, however, the mother may not be able to tell from these rudimentary signals whether the baby is crying from hunger, or colic, or a wet diaper. Only later, as his responses become more specific, will she know what appropriate action to take (Gardner, 1964, p. 91).

After about three weeks it begins to be possible to distinguish between vague agitation and what are clearly distress signals and, since the latter relate increasingly to specific situations, they are relatively easy to identify, provided we are able to observe the situations which prompt them. Bridges continues:

'Cries of distress were heard from month-old babies in the hospital on the following occasions: on waking suddenly from sleep, struggling to breathe through nostrils blocked with mucus, when the ears were discharging, when lying awake before feeding time, after staying long in the same position, lying on a wet diaper, when the child's buttocks were chafed, and when the fingers were rapped. The three main causes of distress at this age, therefore, seemed to be discomfort, pain and hunger.'

These feelings, which are produced in response to internal discomfort or hunger, show several of the conventional characteristics of emotion. There is facial contortion, bodily movement, sharp vocalization, and the suggestion that some strong motivation is being blocked or impeded. What is not clear at this stage is whether there is any conscious awareness on the baby's part of the situation in which he finds himself and, in the absence of such awareness, some psychologists prefer to call these responses 'feelings' rather than 'emotions'. They appear to be simply automatic reactions to internal biological tensions.

It is about the third month that an event occurs which marks perhaps the first true milestone in emotional development. The baby suddenly begins to cry not only when he is hungry or uncomfortable, but also on occasions when he is put down or deserted by his mother or by the person who looks after him. Such crying is an expression of emotion, not feeling, since it evidently depends upon rudimentary conscious operations. The baby, it appears, has become capable of anticipating what the loss of his mother might mean. Repeated satisfactions of his bodily needs have built up expectations associated with his mother's presence and, once the capacity to anticipate pleasure in a particular context has been acquired, it also becomes possible to anticipate 'unpleasure' when the mother goes away (Spitz, 1963). In such a situation the uncertainty is disturbing. For all the child knows the mother may *never* return. This is perhaps the infant's first manifestation of emotion, his first conscious experience of apprehension or uncertainty.

Bayley's (1932) analysis of the causes of crying in infants points to a similar broad sequence of development. She found that during the first two months babies cry mainly because of colic or some other physical discomfort, but that thereafter they also cry when they find themselves in a strange situation or if they are being handled by unaccustomed methods. Here, again, the cause of distress appears to be psychological rather than somatic. The infant could not experience some situations as strange unless he had previously learned to perceive other situations as familiar. The emotion is preceded by an act of perceptual appraisal, as the result of which the baby somehow senses that a change in his situation bodes ill for his welfare.

The expression of delight, which normally appears about the eighth month, also signifies genuine emotion, since it too depends upon conscious appraisal, and relates to some object or situation which the child interprets as being (in this case) favourable to himself and his needs. According to Bridges, the main characteristics of delight include: open eyes and expansion of the face into a smile, as contrasted with the puckering of the forehead and closing of the eyes in distress; welcoming and approaching gestures; responsive vocalizations; and prolonged attention to the object of interest. Of these characteristics, smiling is the one to which parents naturally attach greatest importance. The smiling response proper (as distinct from random activity of the facial muscles, which looks like a smile but is really a discharge phenomenon) normally develops about the third month and, while opinions differ as to whether it is a response to changing expressions in the mother's face (Spitz, 1963), to the demeanour of the person behind the face (Arnold, 1960), or whether it is the infant's specific response to the voice and glance of another human being (Bühler, 1930), the fact remains that it hinges upon processes of perceptual appraisal which are becoming increasingly more specific. Whereas a tiny baby smiles indiscriminately at every adult offering the appropriate pattern of stimulation, after six months smiling is no longer reflexive but highly discriminating: the infant smiles at some persons but not others. He smiles at the faces of those who bring him his bodily satisfactions; he stares vacantly at strangers and may draw away from them.

In the case of delight, the emotion often depends upon anticipating how a particular situation will develop. Consider, for example, a baby's attentive expression while he plays peep-bo with his mother or throws toys out of the pram in the hope that she will return them. Expressions of uncertainty (even apprehension, if the suspense is protracted) then radiant delight flit across his features in rapid succession. His joy consists in successfully anticipating events which bring him closer to his mother and which he also enjoys for their own sake. At eight months of age, as Bridges observes, the child seems to take more delight than ever in self-initiated, purposeful activity. He babbles and splutters and laughs to himself. He is delighted with the noise he makes by banging spoons or other playthings on the table. Whatever brings him into pleasant contact with the world, whatever gives him a chance to reach for, play with, or master things, is eagerly welcomed.

At this age, his range of motivations is clearly extending. The eight-month old infant is activated by curiosity, by a desire to explore and manipulate objects, as well as by his physiological needs and his craving for affection and comfort. At the same time, the *how* of his behaviour is also developing: he is beginning to anticipate events and trying to influence objects which bear upon his desires. Whenever his tentative expectations are sharply disappointed, he cries; if they are gratifyingly and somewhat unexpectedly fulfilled, he smiles happily. Thus, we need to interpret infant emotions in terms of an anticipatory as well as a reactive psychology. Some of the traditional concepts by which classical theories of motivation have sought to explain behaviour – maintenance of equilibrium, tension-reduction, drive-reduction and stimulus-response – imply that the living being is to a large extent, an inert, passive thing waiting to be acted upon. But a baby is not wholly at the mercy of biological push-and-pull mechanisms. It is true that tensions relating to hunger, cold and thirst continue to distress him intermittently, as they will do on and off throughout the rest of his life, but, as he matures, these reactive responses will account for a diminishing range of his affective behaviour. Only under conditions of extreme deprivation – in times of famine, war or pestilence, for instance, when the basic commodities of life are in short supply – will tensions relating to physiological needs be likely to induce strong arousal. There will be minor occasions no doubt when he will kick himself for forgetting the sandwiches, or feel the sort of emotion Jerome's three hungry men in a boat felt when confronted with a tin of pineapple and no tin-opener to get at its contents, but such occasions will probably be rare. As a dweller in modern suburbia he is likely to find that his basic physiological needs (other than sex) will be taken care of almost automatically, or at any rate with little conscious effort upon his part, with the result that they will seldom cause him any serious emotional disturbance. Only when a man is starving does the sight of food make him frenzied.

There are many emotions in fact which cannot be explained in terms of a purely reactive psychology, since they depend wholly upon the anticipation of future events. A child's mounting excitement as he impatiently awaits the arrival of Christmas Day, or his growing apprehension as the appointed hour for visiting the dentist draws near, are cases in point. In both instances there is powerful motivation (the desire for new toys and other good things, the wish to avoid pain) which accounts for the intensity of the emotion, but these feelings are essentially forward-looking ones. What agitates the child who is longing for the arrival of Christmas is that the attainment of his goal is intolerably delayed and there is nothing he can do to accelerate it. During the suspense of waiting, all sorts of doubts and uncertainties may beset his mind: he begins to imagine hazards which may come between him and the realization of his hopes. In the second case the situation is more or less reversed. Instead of time dragging, the hours seem to fly past with winged feet. There is little uncertainty moreover about what the future holds in store (especially if the child has been to the dentist's before): indeed, the fate which lies ahead is all too inevitable. It is this very inevitability, in fact, which gives rise to the emotion. Were the child free to follow his own inclinations, he would have nothing to do with the dentist, but he is not free to decide. He has no resources strong enough to withstand the pressure of his parents' insistence and he cannot avoid the impending situation which hangs over him. And yet, although his parents may talk themselves blue in the face about how much good it will do him to have his tooth out, all he can think of is how much it is going to hurt. Only afterwards is he able to realise that the anticipation was far worse than the actuality.

There is no doubting then the strength of the infant's motivational urges: it is his capacity for executing patterns of behaviour appropriate for realizing his goals which is weak. His cognitions are ill-developed, his adaptive resources are poor and badly co-ordinated. The baby has little knowledge of the world around him, few techniques for controlling it, no anticipation of what it holds in store. He simply registers distress therefore whenever smooth functioning is impeded. When he encounters an obstacle there is very little he can do except cry which, apart from being a call for assistance, is itself an expression of helplessness. A baby placed in too hot a bath cries; an adult adds cold water.

As he develops, however, instead of succumbing to every situation he encounters, the child increasingly makes use of the energy associated with an emotion like anger to try to surmount or get rid of obstacles which he sees as impeding him. But he does not always know how to deal effectively with a frustrating situation. His energy is expended in random, undirected behaviour which, Goodenough (1931) observed, often takes the form of ineffectual jumping up and down, stamping and kicking, throwing himself on the floor, pouting or screaming. The child who is a little older attempts to make some rudimentary assessment of the situation. He tends to make some visible object in the immediate vicinity responsible for his frustration and employs retaliative behaviour upon it; throwing it about, grabbing, pinching, biting, striking, calling it names or arguing (according to age). Again, the adaptive responses are poor and inappropriate: the child may vent his feelings upon a perfectly innocent object, like a piece of furniture or a broken toy. It is not the emotion which is at fault in this case; it is the cognitions that are weak. The true facts of the situation have not been grasped, or the child's interpretation of the facts is incorrect. He believes that the toy itself is perversely responsible for his frustration, not perceiving that it is perhaps his own clumsiness which has caused the toy to break.

While the motives impelling the infant are simpler and less complex than those of the adult, they are, in their own way, equally compelling and equally capable of arousing violent emotion. Where the infant chiefly differs from the grown-up is that he lacks adequate techniques for controlling his emotions: he cannot communicate his feelings effectively, nor has he learnt yet to brook delays or defer satisfaction of his needs. Consequently, his emotional outbursts tend to be highly impulsive, intense and explosive. The pressure is always on him, moreover, in that he is constantly being faced with situations which he has not previously encountered, where he is unsure what the 'correct' response is. Until he acquires better adaptive resources he thus remains peculiarly vulnerable to all those types of situation which most frequently produce emotion in human beings. These situations may be classified as: (1) new situations, for which a person is not

adequately prepared; (2) situations which, even though repeated, are always new in the sense that there is no obviously
'correct' response to them; and (3) situations which are not
new or unusual perhaps, but which develop unexpectedly so
that they catch a person off his guard, so to speak, before
he has had time to readjust to them. Janet (1928) illustrated
this latter type of situation with a pathological example
(quoted by Fraisse, 1968, p. 128). A young woman was waiting
for a piece of furniture which she had ordered and which she
wanted very much. It was delivered sooner than she expected
and, instead of feeling satisfaction, she was very upset. She herself explained: 'If I had been warned, if I had seen the van from
the window, I would not have been upset.' Her experience
explains why, when we wish to spare our friends from sudden
emotion, we usually try to prepare them for bad news, and
sometimes even for intense joy.

At first, everything is strange to the infant, who comes
into the world knowing nothing, entering a universe where
each new stimulus arrives as an unexpected phenomenon.
Gradually, as more things are experienced, the world of object
relations begins to fall into some kind of shape or pattern.
Certain events are discovered to recur with regularity,
certain objects to behave in ways which are constant and
predictable. Thus, the infant begins to 'place' novel sources
of stimulation into some sort of stable pattern or framework,
so that their repetition occasions a steadily diminishing
response.

As intellectual development, learning and experience proceed, the framework of object relations into which each new
experience is fitted becomes more secure. This is possible only
because the world is, to a large extent, constant and predictable. With each advance of knowledge the child acquires
a new reference point by which to distinguish the familiar
from the unfamiliar, and new bearings for shaping his future
behaviour. Objects firmly identified and established in this
way are no longer matters for speculation or guesswork:
repeated experience enables the child to predict how under

given conditions they will behave. If it were not so, he could never make sense of his world. But, in the early years especially, the child's hold on the world of object relations is precarious and unstable: the infant discovers that the familiar is constantly being presented in novel or unfamiliar contexts – a circumstance which can be both intriguing and disturbing. The more deeply grooved a particular object relationship has become, by repetition, the more alarming it may be if it suddenly appears in unaccustomed, variant form. Hebb's (1949, pp. 242–45) study of fear in infant chimpanzees illustrates this point vividly.

Hebb showed chimpanzees of various ages a model of a human or chimpanzee head detached from the body. He found that infant chimpanzees showed no fear of this object, that increasing excitement was evident in half-grown animals, but that adult chimpanzees were either terrified or considerably agitated by it. It was the older animals, in short, who found an unfamiliar variant of the norm most difficult to reconcile with their past accumulated experience. The experiment using detached heads was followed up by others, using various stimuli: an isolated eye and eyebrow, a cast of a chimpanzee's face, a skull, a cured chimpanzee hide, an anaesthetized chimpanzee. Hebb observed that individual responses to these stimuli varied greatly: some animals were afraid or excited, some showed aggression, others displayed apparent friendliness. Sometimes there was a confused mixture of all three reactions, indicating that some animals were not sure how to respond to such ambiguous stimuli.

The agitation produced by these experiments resulted, according to Hebb, from a failure of 'temporal integration' or 'phase sequence' within the neural brain circuits. This is perhaps only another way of saying that well-established expectations suddenly went astray, when the familiar was presented in an unfamiliar context. It is significant that agitation disappeared when animals were exposed repeatedly to these unusual stimuli – repetition, so to speak, having made the unfamiliar familiar. It is the mixture of the known and the unknown in fact which often produces fear, as a further observation of Hebb's illustrates. Hebb (1949, p. 251) writes that '. . . a familiar attendant *A*, wearing the equally familiar coat *B* of another attendant, may arouse fear just as a complete stranger would. *A* causes no disturbance; *B* causes none; *A* and *B* together cause a violent emotional reaction.' One may observe a similar reaction in children. A child may be terrified if his father puts on a mask or false beard, or if he sees the stuffing pulled out of a favourite teddy-bear.

When the familiar is thus juxtaposed with the bizarre, a dislocation of well-grooved expectations occurs which may be frightening. Likewise, fear is often aroused when, as happens at night-time, an unfamiliar sound is heard when a child does not expect it. The branch of a tree taps eerily against the window-pane, the bedroom curtains rustle mysteriously, or there is a sudden commotion inside the chimney where a sparrow has become trapped. The child cannot account for these unexpected noises and, because it is dark, he feels himself cut off from those sources of sensory feedback which normally give him information about the world and enable him to predict how objects in it will behave. In the uncertainty of total darkness a vacuum is created in which fantasies of the imagination – created perhaps out of stories or television material – assume menacing, unrealistic proportions. As stable bearings slip away, emotion is always apt to take over.

Young children are especially vulnerable to emotion because their framework of object relations is unstable and they cannot always distinguish between fantasy and reality. A child can feel genuinely afraid and yet be in no real danger. He may be in no danger but be afraid because he thinks he is, or he may be in danger but be unaware of it and so not be afraid (Kenny, 1963, p. 49). It follows that emotion sometimes arises because children misconceive objects, or because they entertain beliefs which are irrational: they think that a white sheet flapping in the darkness is a ghost, or are convinced that some eccentric old woman is a witch who wants to eat them. The emotion felt in such cases may be said to be inappropriate and unrealistic, since a truer evaluation of all the relevant facts would promptly dispel it.

So far as ordinary events in the physical world are concerned it becomes possible, with experience, to predict their outcomes fairly accurately. We can be reasonably certain for instance, if it is day-time and there are no clouds in the sky, that the sun will be shining. (And yet, if by some bizarre circumstance, this expectation suddenly broke down – as might happen if the sun were unexpectedly eclipsed before the eyes of ignorant savages – then the emotional repercussions would be considerable.) Similarly, after appropriate learning has taken place, we can make confident predictions about things which are symbolically self-evident: for example, that 2 + 2 will always make 4. When it comes to anticipating other people's behaviour however, prediction is always much more difficult. Grown-ups have internalized widely differing sets of beliefs, opinions and so forth, which cause them to approach situations with pre-established attitudes, so that their interpretations of situations vary considerably and in a manner which children, who rely on adults for guidance, find disconcerting. Thus, one child feels guilty about doing something like smoking because his parents have taught him to believe that that action is wrong; another child has no such emotional inhibition because his parents do not share that particular belief. Whereas, in due course of time, it becomes possible to predict everyday physical occurrences fairly accurately, and to arrive at a truer evaluation of all the relevant facts about phenomena like sheets flapping on a clothes line and witches (with the result that emotion is dispelled), a child soon discovers that it is impossible to predict other people's behaviour anything like so accurately. Hence, emotion is constantly breaking out in the sphere of his social relationships.

The late G. A. Kelly, whose *Psychology of Personal Constructs* (1963) represents a bold attempt to devise a wholly new kind of anticipatory psychology, illustrated the sort of complex, inter-related factors which a child may have to take into account in trying to anticipate an adult's response to even the most trivial occurrence:

'A child predicts that if he breaks his mother's necklace he will get a spanking. He seems to perceive an *if-then* relationship between the breakage and the spanking. But this is never a simple one-to-one relationship, even to a child. To predict the spanking it is necessary for him to construe a considerable variety of events: his mother's disposition and mood, the value she places on the necklace, his own part in the breakage, the discovery of his act, a previous spanking or two, and the circumstances which surrounded the previous spankings. From these he abstracts a trend. At one pole of his trend construct are those events which lead away from a spanking; at the other are those which lead toward it. The events now confronting him look like those which lead towards the spanking' (p. 123).

Or consider this story told to me by a colleague, which, in its homely way, tells us a good deal about children's emotions, in terms both of motivation and ability (or inability) to predict and anticipate events involving other people.

'Jane, who is five, had recently learnt to play whist with her family. One day, just before the game started, she was observed to be secretly 'fixing' the cards, arranging them in such a way that when later they were dealt she would be sure to receive a good hand while Mummy and Daddy would receive poor hands. Unbeknown to Jane, her father witnessed and was amused by this action – it certainly demonstrated intelligence – and soon afterwards he found a pretext for getting Jane out of the room. While she was away, the cards were quickly rearranged, so that this time Jane would receive a poor hand, while her parents each received good hands. Jane returned, eyes bright with anticipation, and she dealt out the cards without perceiving that they had been interfered with. When she looked at the cards she had dealt herself she was utterly flabbergasted (the only word adequate to describe her reaction). She did not guess what had happened, but flew into a rage and rushed out of the room, declaring that she would never play cards any more.'

This story illustrates how rapidly emotion can plummet from delight to dismay, when a seemingly sound expectation suddenly and inexplicably misfires.

More will be said in later chapters about the difficulties of adjusting to the belief-systems of other people, especially those from alien cultural backgrounds. For the moment it suffices to say that children are obliged to predict and adjust to the behaviour of others, their own behaviour being governed to a large extent by the way they construe other people's. This creates problems: where two people are not on quite the same wave-length, either from inability to communicate effectively, or from their having developed radically different belief-systems and attitudes, prediction and adjustment tend to be difficult.

Because each child's experience and past history is unique, he perceives and responds to the world in his own peculiarly individual terms. His perceptions are influenced by whatever knowledge he possesses (including the knowledge of his own personal capabilities), by the system of attitudes, beliefs, dispositions and values he has formed, and by how he happens to be motivated at the time. Experiments have shown, for example, that people perceive words more readily if these relate to their own interests or values (Postman, Bruner and McGinnies, 1948); that stereotyped notions of racial characteristics often influence perception; that perception is notably affected by encouragement, or by the promise of reward or punishment. An interesting study by Gilchrist and Nesberg (1952) illustrates the effects of hunger and thirst on perception. They asked college students to refrain from eating for a period of twenty hours and then, just after the times at which they would normally have been taking their meals, they asked them to make perceptual judgments in tests which consisted of matching the brightness of coloured slides containing pictures of T-bone steaks, fried chicken, and so forth. Each slide was presented first at a standard brightness and the students were asked to study it. Then, after a few seconds, the slide was presented again at either a higher or a lower level of brightness, and the students were required to turn a knob to adjust the brightness to match that of the earlier presentation. Alhough the students believed they were making accurate judgements, there was in fact a systematic error: as they became hungrier, they made the pictures of food brighter and brighter. Significantly, control subjects, who had not gone without food, did not show this progressive change. In an analogous experiment, thirsty students also made pictures of iced water, orange juice and other liquids brighter as they became increasingly thirsty. There have been many similar such experiments, demonstrating how perception is influenced by both motivational and cognitive factors.

How a pupil sees an object as affecting himself therefore is not necessarily the way other children or the teacher see it as affecting themselves. In this matter we are all the prisoners of our private subjectivism: our perceptions do not necessarily match those of others nor need they correspond to objective reality. We can make an effort to view the world from another person's standpoint and, children especially, are much influenced by other people's ways of looking at things; but in the last resort each individual is obliged to make what sense he can of the world. Because, in the light of all the variables which govern perception, each of us sees the world so differently, our susceptibility to emotion varies greatly, not only as between person and person, but even in the same person in similar situations at different times. In fact, we probably never see the 'same' situation twice. How I see a situation today is influenced by how I last saw a situation like it. If it produced emotion in me then, the memory of what happened before is likely to influence my appraisal today.

E

As mentioned earlier, there is a sense in which we become less emotional as we grow older and as we develop better resources for handling life's situations. A child normally outgrows his fear of darkness and imaginary creatures, and many of the objects which aroused emotion in him during infancy eventually cease to trouble him. Thus, according to Woodworth (1940): 'A scale for emotional age, after the analogy of the Binet scale for mental age, would consist in large part of tests for *not* being afraid or angry or grieved or inquisitive over things which regularly arouse these emotions in the younger child (p. 432). And yet, as we grow older, our motivations and interests become increasingly complex, with the result that the cues capable of eliciting emotion in us as adults are subtler and more numerous than when we were children. Things like apartheid, the ethics of blood sports, social injustice, abortion, euthanasia, the siting of new airports, the question of how long a young man should grow his hair – all these are matters which can arouse strong emotions in adults, but to which young children may be almost totally indifferent. As we mature, moreover, the range of emotions which potentially we can experience widens, while the emotions themselves become more finely differentiated. This gradual differentiation of emotion is a process which commences in early infancy. A new born baby feels only generalized excitement or quiescence but, by the age of two years (according to Bridges), distress, anger, fear, disgust, jealousy, affection and elation are already clearly distinguishable. How then does one emotion differ from another? Does each emotion develop its own distinctive pattern of physiological characteristics?

This is not an easy question to answer. As everyone knows, some emotions tend to be associated with specific physical sensations – a lump in the throat, a flutter in the stomach, a dry feeling in the mouth, the knees turning to water, and so forth. And there is a palpable difference between the physical feeling of fear (shivers down the spine, hair standing on end, clammy hands, rapidly beating heart) and the feeling we have when we are bubbling over with joy. We would expect, indeed, that emotions would 'feel' different, according to whether they are sympathetically or parasympathetically aroused (see pp. 25-7 above). The question is: are there significant physiological differences between two emotions like anger and fear, both of which are sympathetically aroused? It appears, in fact, that anger and fear reactions do differ slightly in their chemical composition. In anger, it is claimed, the stomach-lining tends to turn red, while in fear or depression it is much paler in colour (Wolf and Wolff, 1943). Anger and fear also appear to differ slightly in the proportions of nor-adrenalin and adrenalin which respectively they secrete (Funkenstein, 1955).

Yet no child learns to differentiate anger from fear because of any introspective awareness he possesses of what is happening to his stomach-lining. The main bodily changes which go on inside him are not very dissimilar whether it is anger or fear he is experiencing (indeed, both reactions are so difficult to distinguish in animals that physiologists use the same word 'rage' to denote both). However, there is never any doubt in a child's *mind* as to whether it is anger or fear he is experiencing, for there is all the difference in the world between the subjective experience of these two emotions. (In anger we are inclined to use the energy building up inside us to attack or overcome whatever it is that is blocking our goal; in fear, we are inclined to use this same energy to avoid or run away from the object.) Support for the idea that emotions are differentiated more by their mental than by their physiological characteristics can be found in an important experimental study by Schachter and Singer (1962), who injected subjects with epinephrine (a hormone which produces sympathetic activation) and found that, by exposing their subjects to different social situations, they could produce in them the very disparate emotional states of euphoria and anger. In each case arousal was stimulated initially by the same hormone injection, but the emotion which resulted was determined by the person's cognitive appraisal of the particular situation to which he was exposed (one situation being deliberately designed to induce anger, the other to induce euphoria).

However much an infant is aware of different physical sensations inside him, these feelings are almost always vague and confused. Not until he acquires language is he able to differentiate them at all precisely. He trembles and runs to his mother and she says 'Don't be frightened', or 'What are you afraid of?' He holds his breath, stamps, pouts, feels the blood rushing to his temples, and she asks 'Why are you so angry?' Thus he learns that in the language of the emotions 'frightened', 'afraid', and 'angry' are appropriate words for labelling those particular kinds of response (Kenny, 1963, pp. 65–7). As he talks and listens to adults, and hears stories read to him about how older people have felt and responded to events, his vocabulary for labelling emotions extends and acquires sharper precision, and it is this developing capacity, wedded to his growing experience of life, which, more than anything else, enables him to discriminate his different emotions.

Here is an example of a story which many mothers read to their children: it is an extract from *The Tale of Two Bad Mice*, by Beatrix Potter. Observe how clearly the different emotions (picked out below in block capitals) are labelled, and how each emotion is connected with a strongly defined situation which brings out its meaning at a level the young child can grasp.

'Tom Thumb and Hunca Munca went upstairs and peeped into the dining-room. Then they squeaked WITH JOY!
Such a lovely dinner was laid out upon the table! There were tin spoons, and lead knives and forks, and two dolly-chairs – all *so* convenient!
Tom Thumb set to work at once to carve the ham. It was a beautiful shiny yellow, streaked with red.
The knife crumpled up and hurt him; he put his finger in his mouth.

"It is not boiled enough, it is hard. You have a try, Hunca Munca."

Hunca Munca stood up in her chair, and chopped at the ham with another lead knife.

"It's as hard as the hams at the cheesemonger's," said Hunca Munca.

The ham broke off the plate with a jerk, and rolled under the table.

"Let it alone," said Tom Thumb; "give me some fish, Hunca Munca!"

Hunca Munca tried every tin spoon in turn; the fish was glued to the dish.

Then Tom Thumb LOST HIS TEMPER. He put the ham in the middle of the floor, and hit it with the tongs and with the shovel – bang, bang, smash, smash!

The ham flew all into pieces, for underneath the shiny paint it was made of nothing but plaster!

Then there was no end to the RAGE AND DISAPPOINT-MENT of Tom Thumb and Hunca Munca. They broke up the pudding, the lobsters, the pears and the oranges.' (pp. 21–30).

I was interested to see how my seven-year old son, who had had this book read to him once before, would respond to the above extract if it were presented to him, in typescript, with the emotional sign-posts having been altered. Thus, for 'LOST HIS TEMPER' I substituted the words 'was pleased', and I changed 'RAGE AND DISAPPOINTMENT' in the last paragraph to 'joy and satisfaction'. (Block capitals were not used in the typescript, as I did not wish to draw attention to the emotional labelling words.) I asked Ian to read the passage and to write down what he thought about it. He scrutinized it for several minutes and then wrote: 'I do not agree about the last sentence of where his satisfation is very graet, anyway I think he is very distucktive.' The reasoning is not entirely cogent perhaps, but the inference is clear. Like any seven-year old of normal reading ability Ian already knew enough about words like 'pleased', 'joy' and 'satisfaction' to recognize when they were being used inappropriately. A seven-year old German boy would be equally knowledgeable presumably about phrases like *'er freute sich'*, *'Glück'* and *'Zufriedenheit'*, the German equivalents roughly of these English expressions.

The words which we make use of for labelling emotions are arbitrary signs by means of which we symbolize different states of subjective awareness. They enable us to make subtle and delicate distinctions among our responses to different situations. Consider, for example, the emotions suggested by words like 'annoyance', 'irritation', 'anger', 'frustration', 'rage', 'fury', 'hostility' and 'enmity'. From the physiologist's point of view these emotions are virtually indistinguishable. Each of them implies some degree of sympathetic arousal, but they cannot be differentiated purely on the criterion of physiological intensity, since a person can be every bit as 'worked up' while experiencing frustration as he would be if he were experiencing anger or rage, while enmity is a deep-seated attitude rather than an emotion, which can lie dormant for long periods without betraying any sign of arousal. Words like 'annoyance', 'irritation', 'rage', 'fury' and 'hostility', some of which are nearly but not quite synonymous, do however enable us to discriminate among qualitatively distinct shades of subjective awareness or 'feeling tone'. With the aid of such words we are able to discuss our private reactions with other people, and to understand and sympathize with their reactions to similar situations. Hence, by developing the verbal capacity to differentiate his emotions the child learns (almost literally, in fact) to come to terms with his feelings and to understand them more fully. He finds that by putting his feelings into words he sometimes gains relief for them, and he discovers that his developing capacity for sharing in the feelings of others binds him more closely to other people in a bond of common kinship and humanity.

We have now reached a point in the discussion where,

having identified some of the basic elements in an emotional response, we can begin to draw attention to those factors in emotional development which are of special interest to the educationist. Emotion is an experience triggered by perception in which a person appraises some object or situation as bearing favourably or unfavourably upon himself and the attainment of his goals. It is a response marked by patterns of physiological change which may be experienced as pleasant or unpleasant. If a child is motivated too strongly in proportion to his potential to handle a situation, then emotional disturbance may result; whereas if, against all the odds as it were, his tentative predictions concerning the outcome of events are gratifyingly fulfilled, then he registers pleasure and delight. When the *why* of behaviour (motivation) and the *how* of behaviour (a person's repertoire of knowledge, adaptive resources, and capacity to predict the outcome of events) – when these two sets of elements function together harmoniously, progress toward the attainment of the desired goal tends to be smooth and unimpeded, and consequently there is little emotion. So far as the day-to-day life of the mature adult is concerned, this smooth, unemotional functioning is indeed the norm rather than the exception, since he can achieve the majority of his goals by executing patterns of behaviour which are almost second nature to him. By reducing things that have to be done to mere routine or habit, he sets his mind free to attend to other things that are more interesting, novel and worth while. With children the case is rather different.

Young children are particularly vulnerable to emotion because they are constantly being surprised by situations for which they are not adequately prepared, or for which they simply do not know what the 'correct' response is. Their knowledge of the world and of social relationships is slender and insecure: hence, they frequently misconceive objects or fail to distinguish adequately between fantasy and reality, while many of their beliefs are entirely irrational. As they acquire greater competence in dealing with the environment however, things which formerly aroused emotion in them gradually lose their potency. They become more tolerant of minor frustrations and delays, learning to control and express their emotions better and, at the same time, developing the capacity to enter more and more into the feelings of others. Yet, as their motivations grow more complex and sophisticated, and as their social disposition and range of interests extend outwards, the variables which govern each child's way of looking at the world and the sorts of cues capable of eliciting emotion in him become more subtly individualized, so that it becomes increasingly difficult to predict or anticipate what any given child's emotional response to a particular situation will be.

In this brief account of the child's emotional life certain elements have been passed over which are normally regarded as fundamental and crucial in emotional development. There has been no mention, for example, of the tender intimacy of the mother-child relationship, nor of the role of breast-feeding which, traditionally, has been invested with a sacred, almost mystical, force. The child's deep need of love and affection, and the emotional effects of maternal deprivation have likewise scarcely been touched upon (which seems odd in a book that purports to deal with children's emotions). It would have been interesting, for example, to consider some of the implications of Harlow's (1959) experiments in rearing young rhesus monkeys with 'wire dummy mothers', and to have looked into the question of whether a strong bond of affection between mother and infant is indispensable for normal emotional development. These topics have been excluded not because they are regarded as being in any sense unimportant: indeed, in the present writer's view, one cannot place too high a value upon the loving care which a mother provides, and for which there is probably no adequate substitute. As the researches of John Bowlby (1951, 1970) and other workers in this field indicate, there appear to be critical phases in children's development when a strong bond of attachment to a single mother figure, capable of giving the child love, protection and comfort, is indispensable.

However, it is the parents' and not the teacher's function to provide the physical love and affection the child needs, and the dividing line between their respective functions needs to be carefully drawn. Naturally, the teacher is not indifferent to what goes on in the child's home: because he has a positive interest and concern in the child's emotional problems he accepts that the existence of poor home conditions may make extra demands upon him. If parent or child choose to confide in him about the nature of these problems he will listen sympathetically, for in this way he may to some extent get on the 'inside' of the child's attitudes and feelings. While he has no right to intrude or meddle in other people's domestic affairs he recognizes that these play a formative part in the child's education, since events occur outside school, especially during the foundational modelling of infancy, which leave indelible traces on the child's subsequent emotional development and which may indeed counteract much of what the teacher is trying to do for the child. Deeply ingrained, emotionally charged attitudes take root in the intimate atmosphere of the home which may endure, relatively unchanged, for a lifetime (Peck and Havighurst, 1960, pp.106ff.). It is with regard to these aspects of the child's emotional behaviour – his cognitions, beliefs, attitudes and values, as well as with regard to his physical skills and adaptive resources – that the teacher, in his role as instructor, is principally concerned. But (as will be explained more fully in Chapters 4 and 5) the techniques of persuasion employed need to be carefully and sensitively handled. The aim is always that the pupil should be encouraged to reflect upon his own attitudes and beliefs, not be coerced into surrendering them. To assail these attitudes by direct, open confrontation is to run the risk of undermining the child's whole belief-system and to invite a degree of emotional disturbance which may be more than he can bear.

Apart from the physical affection which the mother gives

her child there is another aspect of the mother-infant relationship which points forward to the role which the teacher can play in affective education. The mother, it needs emphasizing, provides not only love and protection, but also a secure base of psychological operations from which the child draws confidence to explore the world around him. She caters for both the conservative and the more outgoing urges which, it was suggested earlier (see pp. 24ff, above), are basic to his nature. She gives him security and at the same time she prompts and encourages his natural adventurousness, acting as a friendly ally and co-explorer in investigating the new environment. She manipulates objects for his pleasure, she presents new problems for him to solve, and she talks to him on a level which he can understand and imitate. He needs the comfort which mothering gives him, but equally he needs this invigorating contact with his mother's mind. The two elements often blur together inseparably, since the mother's tokens of affection, as well as being demonstrations of love, also imply recognition, acceptance or approval of how the child is behaving (just as, conversely, her raised voice or frown signify disapproval). The cognitions, attitudes and behaviours to which these tokens of approval or disapproval relate, count for as much in the long run as the signs of affection themselves, since they will probably persist long after the memory of physical endearments has faded.

It is with the child's outgoing, rather than with his more conservative tendencies, that the teacher is chiefly concerned, although both tendencies have to be reckoned with at all times and particularly in the earliest stages of education. A child entering school for the first time, especially one who has had little contact with other children of his own age, is apt to feel frightened in the crowded, noisy, unfamiliar environment of the classroom. He does not know the 'correct' responses to the demands being made upon him, and he has difficulty in adjusting his behaviour because he cannot construe accurately what is expected of him by the strangers with whom he is surrounded. Because he cannot predict or control

events with any great confidence, his whole belief-system
appears to be in jeopardy, a fact which may give rise to
anxiety and quite irrational fears. Faced with this problem
the reception-class teacher does not begin by correcting or
instructing the child: the first task is to provide security and
protection. An imaginative attempt has to be made to see the
world through the child's eyes, so that the impingement of
potentially frightening stimuli or threats to the child's
confidence can be cushioned or forestalled. Thus, nursery
teachers often find it helpful to allow the mother to remain
with the child in the nursery group for a time, until he feels
ready to let her go. They allow him to bring along a favourite
teddy-bear from home, or, if it gives him comfort, to keep
his coat and hat on in the nursery. He clings to his coat, not
because he needs it to keep warm, but because it represents
a tangible source of 'familiarity' in an unfamiliar environment
(Gardner, 1964, p. 237), and the wise teacher recognises it as
such.

Once basic trust has been established the need for protection gradually recedes, as dependency gives way to the
intrinsic urge to explore the new environment. But the strong
urge toward growth, maturity and independence never wholly
supplants those factors in the child's nature which make him
wish to remain protected and dependent. He alternates between
wanting to experiment, to predict and control events for himself, and desiring to be protected from intolerable degrees
of stress and anxiety. Perceptive teaching consists in helping
the child to reconcile his alternating needs – in preserving a
balance between that degree of anxiety or tension which is
desirable, and that which may become unbearable or abnormal
if not effectively dispelled.

# 4 Emotion in the classroom

A person's reactions to a situation depend, as we have seen, on how he appraises that situation in relation to himself, and on any expectations he brings to bear upon it. Suppose that a child accidentally falls into a deep canal with no one near to assist him. A pattern of physical changes ensues as his sympathetic nervous system mobilizes the body's resources to cope with the emergency. His heart beats more rapidly, his breathing quickens, his eye-pupil dilates to improve perception, and various other bodily changes occur in a general transformation of energy level. Let us suppose that the child is a strong swimmer. A succession of subjective states may pass rapidly through his mind – shock, dismay, anxiety, momentary hope as he perceives some steps leading out of the water, a determination to rescue himself. He swims over to the steps and pulls himself out of the water. He feels relieved, even a little pleased with himself at having overcome the danger unaided. But his clothes are wet and cold; he is annoyed at having been so careless; he feels apprehensive about what his parents may say to him when he gets home.

For a child who cannot swim, the situation and the pattern of responses are different. Again there is intense excitation of the sympathetic nervous system, but, because no immediate escape from the danger seems possible, fear persists. The child threshes about in unavailing panic or is paralysed with fright. He sees the steps but despairs of ever reaching them. His subjective state is unenviable. If however the circumstances are altered slightly (by the fortunate accident of there being a life-belt within reach in the water), his expectations and emotional responses will probably be different. This illustrates that the circumstances in which emotions are elicited are crucial for determining whatever emotions are felt. If a child is confident that he can deal with a situation – from having met its like before, from possessing some relevant expertise (like being able to swim) for dealing with it, or from possessing the knowledge that things like life-belts have enabled other people to escape from similar predicaments – then the fear is lessened and his behaviour is shaped accordingly.

We may suppose that after this experience the non-swimmer would in future keep well away from deep water, his behaviour being motivated by fear. A shrewd observer might nevertheless suspect that he was afraid of water, because of the many stratagems and pretexts he invented for avoiding it. To prove the point he might take the boy to the water's edge and there record his heart rate and psycholgalvanic reflexes. The readings would probably be high but, as Kenny (1963, pp. 35–37) explains, they would not be a natural manifestation of the boy's fear for, in placing him there against his will, the experimenter would have deprived the boy's fear of its most natural expression – the evasive devices. Thus, we can judge the intensity of an emotion, Kenny suggests, either by the violence of the bodily changes which accompany it, or by the extent to which it governs a person's voluntary actions over a period of time, this second criterion being sometimes the more reliable.

By means of this distinction we can thus differentiate between *aroused emotion* and what may loosely be called an *emotional attitude* (or 'latent' emotion, as some writers prefer to call it). It is a useful distinction and one which has considerable significance for affective education. An aroused emotion is necessarily short-lived, for the bodily changes which accompany it depend upon a sudden transformation of energy level which cannot continue for long before the counter-balancing mechanisms of the autonomic nervous system begin to cancel it out (see p. 27 above). Emotional arousal can recur therefore, but it cannot endure for any great length of time. An emotional attitude, on the other hand, can persist so as to influence a person's future behaviour over a long period of time, and this type of emotional manifestation is, consequently, of great interest to the educator. Whatever it is that persists in an emotional attitude it must be some subjective element, involving cognition and memory, which is capable of influencing future behaviour: and this is more or less what happens. 'Attitude' is not an easy word to define but, for our purposes, an emotional attitude may be regarded as an enduring tendency or disposition to react emotionally whenever a certain object or type of situation presents itself. For long periods it lies dormant or latent, but, whenever stimulated by the appropriate set of circumstances, emotional arousal tends to recur, and with each recurrence of arousal the emotional attitude becomes more deep-rooted.

This loose definition of what constitutes an emotional attitude incorporates two elements which, although logically distinguishable, tend in practice to become psychologically blurred, these elements being: (1) the *memory* of previous experiences, and (2) certain structural *dispositions*. In their recent discussion of this vexed matter, Magda Arnold devotes attention chiefly to the former while Lazarus emphasizes the latter. Thus, Arnold (1970), describing the role played by 'affective memory' in the formation of emotional attitudes, writes:

'Intuitive appraisal is greatly influenced and on occasion even determined by affective memory. This is particularly striking when the original experience has been very intense. A child that has been bitten by a dog may avoid dogs for a long time, whether he remembers the incident later or not. But even if the original experience has not been so intense but [the] child or adult has had many similar experiences, his appraisal of such situations is biased more and more because affective memory gradually hardens into an attitude of acceptance or rejection. Such attitudes, based on affective memory, are indispensable for our daily living:

if we had to wait until something actually harmed us before we could appraise it as bad and avoid it, the survival rate of man and animal would drop alarmingly.

Since affective memory is a reliving of the original acceptance or rejection in a new though similar situation, the resulting feeling carries no date line so that we are completely unaware that our here-and-now appraisal is really a prejudgement (literally, a prejudice) dictated by affective memory.' (p. 176).

This explanation of how remembered arousal can harden into an enduring attitude fits Arnold's case of the child bitten by a dog, or the non-swimmer's persistent fear of water, described above, but it does not account for the kind of aversion we can feel for things which we have never actually experienced at first-hand. For example, a youngster who has never smoked a cigarette (and hence has no memory of such an experience) can feel a strong aversion to smoking because, on the basis of what his father or a report by the Royal College of Physicians has decreed, he judges smoking to be an undesirable activity. Apart from those attitudes stemming from previous experience therefore, individuals also develop value-determined attitudes which pre-suppose systems of moral or ethical judgement (Bedford, 1957), and these attitudes are usually socially or culturally acquired.

Then, too, there are biological factors which contribute to the development of psychological dispositions. We inherit certain adjustments to regularities in our environment: phylogenesis disposes us to respond to certain types of stimuli in a biologically adaptive fashion which contributes to our own survival or that of the species (Lazarus *et al.*, 1970). These inherited psychophysical constancies interweave with our acquired attitudes, and become integrated within the structure of the personality (Krueger, 1928). On the basis of all these attitudes and dispositions, the combined product of experiential, cultural and phylogenetic development, our whole outlook upon the world, and our estimation of what are the most significant realities in our lives, are moulded. And, as Krueger suggests, if ever these structural dispositions are threatened, or come into serious conflict one with another, we feel shaken to the very core of our being. We feel that our entire existence as individuals is at stake.

Thus (bearing in mind what was said earlier about repetition of experience tending normally to diminish emotion) we can see why it is that some classes of object can continue to arouse emotion in us no matter how often we encounter them. The crux of this matter lies, of course, in the nature of the object in question. Some of the most important things in our lives – our children, our friends, the abstract values and ideals we live by – can never be fully comprehended by us in the predictable, totally unambiguous way that inanimate physical objects can be. We react emotionally to these objects in a variety of ways therefore, according to the ever-changing circumstances in which they happen to be viewed. Thus, a mother's attitude to her child varies constantly: she is cross with him when he is naughty, she is anxious when he is sick, she sympathizes with his injuries, she rejoices in his triumphs, and she springs to his defence if anyone else dares to criticize him. Each of these different reactions springs from a common basic impulse or dispositional tendency which never significantly alters nor diminishes.

The objects to which emotional attitudes relate can likewise evoke feelings of antipathy or aversion. (The pathological fear of spiders, bats, dirt, or of the sight of human blood are obvious examples.) They include all those objects concerning which people form deep-seated prejudices or obsessions, also the various types of situation to which a person cannot learn to adjust himself (situations such as being alone, speaking in public, travelling in a lift, being enclosed, and so on). Sometimes it is fear which chiefly characterizes the emotional attitude; sometimes it is jealousy, infatuation or hatred, or a mixture of several emotions, depending upon the nature of the object in question and the circumstances in which it happens to be viewed.

The strength of feeling underlying such attitudes is so powerful that it is easy to overlook the fact that they are often linked to quite rational considerations. This rationality may be pathologically warped in some instances, but this is by no means always the case. A mother's emotional attitudes to her child, for example, are normally based on a reasonable evaluation of what is good for him. Her fondness may tempt her to give in to his desires – to allow him all the sweets he wants and to let him stay up longer than he should – but she knows that such indulgence is not in his true interests and, although, as she says, this hurts her as much as it hurts him, she exercises her discretion and denies him his wishes if she thinks it wiser to do so. Similarly, the person who is afraid to go near deep water, because he once nearly drowned in it, has reasonable grounds for his fear. Although, in taking such evasive action, he is acting out of fear, he is nevertheless acting rationally, for he is doing his best to ensure that at least he will never die by drowning.

Not all emotional attitudes stand up well to rational scrutiny however. We all of us have some emotional skeletons in our cupboards which, if we could only view them dispassionately, or through the eyes of another person, we would recognize as being totally irrational – not basically different from the attitude of the young child who believes that the eccentric old woman at the end of the street is a witch who wants to capture and eat him. While such an irrational attitude persists, the person is apt to re-experience emotional arousal every time he comes into contact with the object to which it relates. But – and this needs to be emphasized – it is the faulty misconception, not the emotion, which is the cause of the trouble. The arousal recurs simply because an unrealistic set of cognitions keeps triggering it off, and it will go on recurring until something happens to modify or improve the cognitions which are prompting it.

Because the emotion seems so persistent, and because it

F

tends to be the most obtrusive factor in every example of maladaptive behaviour, it may blind us to the real cause of the problem. By a long-standing tradition, dating back at least as far as to Plato, we are accustomed – as two of my students' definitions of emotion suggest (see p. 15 above) – always to blame emotion as the cause of irrationality. This, R. S. Lazarus (1966, pp. 250–51) submits, is to confuse cause and effect, the real culprit being the perceptual appraisal, the antecedent dispositions and cognitions (beliefs, expectations, evaluations, learning and memory) which determine the emotional reaction. The reaction is irrational only because it is based on incorrect facts, or on an incorrect assessment of the facts. To blame emotion is to blame the wrong factor therefore, and to seek to 'release' such emotion (as many therapeutically inclined teachers seek to release it) is merely to provide temporary, incidental relief, to treat the symptoms rather than the root problem. It is the antecedent factors which influenced the appraisal that need to be corrected. It need hardly be added that to encourage children to assess the facts of a situation correctly, and to help them form rational attitudes and beliefs, is as much a part of the teacher's traditional function as to transmit socially approved attitudes and values.

This is not to imply that the aim of affective education is purely to get rid of emotion, for no teacher who properly understands its significance would want to banish emotion from the classroom (although he might wish he were more expert at identifying and interpreting it). We have noted already that infant expressions of emotion have a useful signalling function – in the case of crying, as a sign of helplessness or an appeal for help, which has obvious survival value. Indeed, it is this signalling function which, from the educationist's point of view, constitutes one of the most valuable attributes of emotion. Through emotion we communicate something about ourselves to others, and by interpreting other people's emotional signals we learn something about them, on the basis of which we try to anticipate what they will do next. It is mainly by means of his non-verbal affective signals that a child indicates to the teacher, albeit unconsciously, that his belief-system or adaptive resources are being stretched, and it is largely on the basis of these signals that the teacher decides whether correction, guidance or encouragement are needed. If we observe a child carefully, we can usually tell when he is under stress, while there is no mistaking the look of triumph on his face when he first succeeds in performing unaided some difficult task like tying his own shoe-laces or riding a bicycle. Were it not for the guidance which non-verbal cues constantly provide, the teacher might find it difficult to attune to the individual child's particular wave-length and to decide what kind of remedial action is appropriate.

Someone is reported to have said recently at a conference on 'The Education of Emotion' that children should be taught emotional control by being trained 'at brain level to stop sending out irrational emotional signals'. It is even said that with the aid of antibiotics and drugs we could, provided we acted quickly enough, eradicate all memory traces of a disturbing emotional experience. David Krech (1968) and his associates at the University of California actually visualize a time when the biochemist and the teacher, combining their insights and skills, might employ 'memory-repellers' like puromycin on children to prevent their remembering undesirable experiences. Yet, assuming such procedures were employed upon children, what would they achieve? By preventing the transmission of emotional signals we should debar the teacher from a source of information about the child which he needs. By removing the incentive from the child to modify or revise his own cognitions and attitudes we should probably do positive harm. When a child fails to make an appropriate response to a critical situation, and feels his heart skip a beat or experiences a sinking feeling in his stomach, emotion is warning him that some better adaptation is needed to integrate the how and the why of his behaviour. When his spirits lift up and he feels like tossing his cap in the air, emotion is confirming that all's right with his world. Emotional development requires, in fact, that there shall be occasional agitation, out of which better adaptations can grow. Such agitation is not something we could manage better without, or something to be thankfully outgrown. It is a signal which gives us valuable information about ourselves and, as Young (1961, pp. 463–65) observes, people will listen to emotion where no amount of reasoning could persuade them.

As children in school learn new facts and skills they are constantly making predictions and testing these out against reality and experience. Will all this liquid go into this test-tube? How long will this cake need in the oven? Is this the answer the teacher expects? Is he in a good mood this morning? The teacher on his side is making his own predictions. Have I too much or too little material for this lesson? Are they all capable of grasping this point? Will Johnny be interested in this? Is this story suitable for these children? Some of the predictions on both sides can be tested empirically: the liquid will either go into the test-tube or it will spill over; the pupils' grasp of a particular conceptual point can be tested. But the accuracy of some of the other predictions can be judged only by inference, based on observation of facial expression and other non-verbal cues. These signals are sometimes misleading but (as will be demonstrated more fully in Chapter 6) they are the ones which we ordinarily make use of in life and they enable us to make fairly reliable predictions, provided we know the other person reasonably well and have some insight into the situation inducing the response.

The fact that, as a teacher, you cannot always precisely identify an emotion does not mean that you are powerless to influence it, but only that where the child's emotional life is concerned you are obliged sometimes to proceed more in hope or in trust than in certainty. By enlarging and developing the range of the pupil's cognitions, by teaching him new physical skills, by developing his verbal capacities and social confidence, and by encouraging him to reflect upon and evaluate his own attitudes and beliefs, you are bound to influence his later emotional life, since you have affected his appraisal of future situations. But there is no way of gauging the full extent of your influence. In consequence of your teaching, emotions may be generated on some later occasion which, but for your influence, the child would never have experienced or, conversely, the onset of a particular emotion may be avoided which, otherwise, he would probably have felt. For example, by teaching a child proficiency in swimming you ensure that, should he ever chance to fall into deep water, he will appraise the situation from a swimmer's instead of a non-swimmer's standpoint (so influencing his emotional arousal). Likewise, your instruction has obviated any need on his part to invent pretexts for avoiding deep water (so preventing the development of an undesirable emotional attitude). Either way you have plainly influenced the child's subsequent emotional life, but there is of course no way of measuring emotions which never manifested themselves and, in any case, the most critical demonstration of the effectiveness of your teaching (the testing of it in a real life situation) may occur only after the child has left school, in which case you may never even hear about it.

It will be apparent from what has so far been said that science and the practical subjects have, potentially at least, a larger role to play in affective education than that which is traditionally accorded to these subjects. The humanities are commonly regarded as the major vehicle for educating emotion and few writers in this field ever stress the desirability of influencing children's emotions through means of practical activities. It is more customary to regard science and the practical subjects as having no direct bearing upon a pupil's emotions, except in so far as they are capable of providing some elusive quality of aesthetic experience. Mathematics is esteemed as an affective subject only to the limited extent that an elegant proof can be aesthetically pleasing; we esteem Science as a means of influencing emotion only in so far as it can evoke the wide-eyed wonder of young Newtons counting pebbles along the sea-shore. Handiwork and Craft are valued, not so much because they satisfy the intrinsic urge to make and do but, all too often, because they can be invested with the romance of the wheelwright's shop – with emotions, that is to say, which are not typical of young children.

In questioning this sort of approach I do not wish to imply that children should never experience anything beyond the merely practical satisfaction of making and doing. They should come to realise that some ways of manipulating objects are more pleasing than others. We want them to appreciate that materials differ not only in serviceability, but in more delicate qualities of colour, grain and texture, which make some more intrinsically appealing than others. They should be given opportunities 'to know the best that has been done in art or craft' (Jeffreys, 1962, p. 132). There seems little danger however of such considerations being neglected by English educationists: indeed, it is much more likely that an over-preoccupation with these will lead to a restricted view of affective education. This is roughly where we stand at the present time, when the affective potential of a school subject tends to be estimated largely in proportion to its aesthetic significance. Yet there are grounds for thinking that aesthetic emotion may be a comparatively late addition to the child's emotional repertoire. It appears to develop much later than the primary emotions associated with success or failure in achieving basic motivational goals, and as Margaret Phillips (1937, pp. 305–6) observed: 'If the way is to be cleared for genuine aesthetic experience, urgent personal needs in the practical world must be first satisfied. Otherwise such needs will wrest to their own purposes all experience offered, whether potentially aesthetic or otherwise'. By placing our emphasis initially upon the child's primary needs and interests we imply that science and the more practical subjects should be recognized not (as at present) as Cinderella subjects standing on the periphery of the affective field, but as subjects capable of playing a central part in the education of emotion.

Before going on to discuss ways in which practical education can influence emotion, some brief exploration of the nature of aesthetic experience seems called for. Unfortunately this is yet another matter on which major differences of opinion exist, there being considerable disagreement as to whether the aesthetic response does in fact contain any emotional ingredient. Clearly, the pleasure which we derive from looking at works of art or objects of natural beauty is unlike the pleasure we derive from eating or making love, since it is more detached and disinterested. We can appreciate beauty in an object without regard to whether this object has any practical utility for us, and regardless of our material needs. We can enjoy sadness in tragedy, in music, or in a novel like *Tess of the D'Urbervilles*, in a way that we never enjoy sadness in real life. The aesthetic response to tragedy, Pepita Haezrahi (1954) remarks, is not 'Ah, how sad it is' but 'Ah, how beautiful it is' (pp. 40–46).

One reason why it is so difficult to determine the nature of the emotion involved in an aesthetic response is that in seeking information on this matter one is obliged to rely upon other people's introspective recollection of what aesthetic experience is like, and no two people's recollections are ever quite the same. Trying to describe aesthetic experience is almost as difficult as trying to describe pain, for there is nothing else quite like it. Some witnesses claim that, for them, the aesthetic response involves a sense of wonder, awe or sympathy; that it produces intense physiological reactions; that it induces a state of heightened awareness or positive ecstasy. Valentine, in *The Experimental Psychology of Beauty* (1962), quotes a musical artist as saying: 'If I am really in the aesthetic ecstasy, I am absolutely oblivious of my surroundings' (p. 313). Others object that any emotions felt during aesthetic experience are purely incidental: that they arise from extraneous associations, from 'sentimental reveries', or from the misguided habit of reading human feelings into every piece of music or work of art one comes across. According to Susanne Langer (1953, pp. 395–402), good art undoubtedly articulates and presents human feelings to our understanding – and it thus serves to 'educate' emotion – but the response to art is itself primarily intellectual. We enjoy art, Langer suggests, because it clarifies and makes coherent what in ordinary life is confused, intertrammeled and conflicting. Haezrahi (p. 33) agrees: maintaining that the response to art is, or should be, intellectual, intuitive, contemplative, and quite uncontaminated by emotional interference.

Another question of considerable interest to the educator, and on which there is as yet no consensus of agreement, is whether, as Read (1943) and Piaget (1953) maintain, aesthetic sensitivity is a natural propensity of childhood – one which formal education tends all too readily to distort – or whether it is something which is learnt through social and cultural experience. There is no doubt that the aesthetic response does develop with experience, for our tastes certainly change as we grow older. Tchaikovsky or Rossini is perhaps our first love in music, Sibelius or Bruckner our last love. Aesthetic responses are also to some extent culturally shaped. For example, Asiatic music often sounds disagreeable on first hearing to the European ear, although it may become increasingly enjoyable through familiarization (Valentine, p. 225). This raises the question whether it is familiarity which promotes aesthetic enjoyment, since, where works of art are concerned, repetition undoubtedly serves to deepen the response (the more of Bach we hear, the more we enjoy his music). Yet with objects of natural beauty it appears to be some element of surprise or unexpectedness which brings a catch to the throat. It is the first cuckoo in spring, the first daffodil, the first blaze of pink blossom which delights us and prompts us to write to *The Times*. The second, third and fourth cuckoo scarcely merit attention.

There is not space here to pursue the analysis of aesthetic experience – a task to which I hope to return on a future occasion. For the present, it suffices to say that, while teachers should certainly encourage children to enjoy music and art – these activities being valuable in themselves and justifiable on a number of grounds – we should perhaps be cautious about making too much of the role they can play in emotional development until we understand more clearly what this role is. If there is an emotional factor in aesthetic experience, it may turn out to be rather different from other emotions, to be *sui generis*, in fact. We certainly need to know more than we do about the workings of this particular emotion before making the pursuit of it our principal objective in affective education, and meanwhile there are other ways in which teachers can influence children's emotions.

Subjects like science, geography, environmental and rural studies, economics, engineering, woodwork, metalwork, craft, domestic science and PE, which influence the child's orientation to the world, which deepen his understanding of object relationships, and teach him effective skills and techniques for handling problems set by the physical environment – all these subjects have, potentially at least, some bearing upon emotion. Their influence may be argued inferentially, I think, rather than by lengthy enumeration of the various items in a particular subject syllabus which could conceivably affect a pupil's emotions.

There is no doubt that with growing ability to predict and control events comes confidence. If we can handle life's situations competently, we enjoy doing so; if we can't, we worry and fret, or we take evasive action whenever certain situations loom up before us. In the one case, energy is utilized for our own on-going purposes; in the other it tends to be dissipated in involuntary behaviour which we might do better without. This suggests that there is both a positive and a negative sense in which the benefits of practical education can be conceived.

Positively, practical education strengthens the 'how' of behaviour, making a child more knowledgeable about the world he lives in, more self-sufficient and autonomous; it gives him the satisfaction of having the efficiency of his adaptive resources tested and improved. To be able to do things for himself (or herself) – to light a fire, cook, sew, knit, paint, tie a knot, make a joint, solder a pipe, apply a bandage, climb a rope, grow fruit and vegetables, conduct an experiment, do simple household repairs, check a grocery bill, or budget for a household – is to become less dependent and to satisfy the intrinsic urge to control the environment. It is a source of genuine delight to a child when he first succeeds in mastering any of the skills which adult life demands, and so extends his capacity to predict and control external circumstances. The keen satisfaction such mastery brings shows clearly in the testimony of this industrial apprentice, writing about his training under the Outward Bound scheme (James, 1957):

'... above all, you come in at the start of the course as a boy and return at the end of it a man. You are able to be trusted to command a cutter, take the wheel of a ketch, lead your watch in the hills, get cold, damp and miserable and yet still enjoy yourself' (p. 76).

On the negative side, inability to perform the simple skills necessary for realizing his basic goals renders a person more liable to emotional stress. In a world like ours people at some time or other will need to know how to use a telephone, mend a fuse, negotiate traffic, and understand things like decimal currency, metric weights, the centigrade scale, income tax or sickness-benefit forms. Inability to meet these everyday requirements of modern living can lead to anxiety or embarrassment. The disconsolate dependency of the elderly or those suddenly disabled, whose capacity to do things for themselves is impaired, stands in direct contrast to the delight and satisfaction which a child experiences in developing a healthy autonomy.

Children themselves, as Jersild (1946) observes, are often eager to come to grips with fears and anxieties that impede their everyday activities and they welcome instruction which enables them to overcome these. Parents err therefore if they choose to ignore these fears, or try to talk children out of them, or to get rid of them by bribery, ridicule or physical compulsion. The best means of counteracting emotional stress is not by verbal precept or reassurance, but by developing the child's competence for dealing with whatever it is that is arousing apprehension. He needs to be shown, by personal example if necessary, what is the correct adaptive behaviour to the feared situation and, by degrees, be given active experience in facing it. By means of this practical kind of approach Holmes (1936) showed how children could be induced to overcome their fear of going alone into a dark room. The experiment did not prove that the children had overcome their fear of darkness permanently, but Holmes' findings, as far as they go, certainly have significant practical implications. After once entering a dark room, unaccompanied and without hesitation, the child is on the way to overcoming his apprehension. After further repetition of the experience, he will eventually reach a stage where it causes him little emotional agitation.

In the nature of things there is a limit of course to the extent to which children can participate directly in stressful situations in school. It is mainly outside school that such situations are encountered and, much as we might wish to escape from the classroom occasionally (in the way that educational innovators like Kurt Hahn and Mackenzie recommend), this is difficult for staff and pupils in the urban state school, except during weekend or vacation expeditions. Nevertheless, if an imaginative attempt is made to relate practical education to children's real life concerns, they will perceive that the knowledge and skills they acquire in school have a significance which goes beyond the immediate present, and beyond the satisfaction of merely achieving good marks or examination success. If what is taught in science and the craft subjects is *not* seen by the pupil as having this kind of relevance and significance, one wonders what adequate justification there can be for teaching it. As the Newsom

Report emphasizes, 'An Education that Makes Sense' to
secondary-school boys and girls is one that is 'practical' and
'realistic'. The Report defines time spent on practical subjects
as 'time spent away from the classroom and its desks' and as
including art, music and physical education as well as wood-
or metalwork, rural studies, housecraft and needlework.
Newsom continues:

> 'This yardstick will do well enough as an indication of the
> way our minds are working, and, which is perhaps more
> important, the way in which the boys and girls feel.
> Practical, then, when applied to work tends to mean doing
> something where physical skill is needed to produce ends
> which may be as entirely different as throwing a javelin,
> building a rope bridge, budding a rose, making a table,
> painting a picture, singing a descant or baking a cake.
> Usually it leads to something which can be seen or handled,
> though this test will not apply easily to music or drama.
> Apart from the sheer joy which most people feel in making
> something, the special importance of practical work to the
> boys and girls of our report is that it is for many of them
> both the surest way in which to achieve some success and
> the area in which success is best recognized by their peers
> and their parents. The radio works, the canoe floats, the
> dress fits, the top of the mountain was reached. Practical
> work leads not only to success which is easily recognized,
> but to success which is obviously worth while' (para. 318).

'Realistic' is defined by Newsom as a word that has some
affiliation with 'practical', but which is applied more particularly to 'situations in which people find themselves'. To boys
and girls it means simply 'belonging to the real world'.

The person who is well adjusted to the demands of his
physical environment appears to have his emotions well under
control, even in the face of the most intimidating challenge,
as was well illustrated by the American astronauts on their
first mission to the moon. Paradoxically, ordinary persons
watching televised pictures of the original moon-landing pro-

bably became more agitated during this mission than the participants themselves. The explanation of this paradox is not difficult to discover. The astronauts had built up such confidence in their capabilities, from having tested them out in simulated conditions beforehand, that they did not doubt their ability to control events. Thus, they experienced emotion only at what where known beforehand to be critical junctures in their mission – moments when things could go wrong because unknown factors were involved. The earth-bound mortal, who has had none of this special training, has little insight into the workings of the astronaut's thought processes. His imagination tends to magnify the risks which are being taken, and he invests the whole enterprise with a higher degree of emotional suspense than is experienced by the persons actually involved in it.

For some people the astronauts' flat unemotionality was not only astonishing, but somehow repellent. To snuff out emotion in this matter-of-fact way, at the very moment when a centuries-old dream was about to be realized, seemed more like robot than human behaviour. Were we breeding a new race of emotional zombies? One can sympathize with the concern underlying this point of view, and at the same time observe that it was totally unfounded. As was shown during the dramatic Apollo 13 moon mission – which also set itself the task of predicting every eventuality, and thereby forestalling the onset of unwanted emotion – once unforeseen contingencies arose, which upset prior calculations and imperilled the whole enterprise, the astonauts, Lovell, Swigert and Haise, revealed unmistakable signs of emotion.* The first indication came in Lovell's 'Hey, we've got a problem here', as the spacecraft began to gyrate and an oxygen-gauge reading fell to zero. 'Why the hell are we manoeuvring?' Haise demanded. 'I can't take that doggone roll out,' Lovell replied. There followed a rapid exchange of technical information between Apollo 13 and Ground Control. Once the immediate emergency was successfully overcome, Mission Control became

*The same was true, to a lesser extent, during the Apollo 14 mission.

more reassuring: 'You guys are in great shape all round. Why don't you quit worrying and go to sleep?' But the world at large refused to believe that everything was in great shape, for, as the *Guardian* headline (16 April 1970) emotively put it, the spacecraft was 'limping home in hope and fear'. Not surprisingly, the astronauts found it difficult to sleep, for by this time they knew that their lives were in jeopardy. In a press interview afterwards Lovell explained how his worries had increased all the time: 'I went from "I wonder what this is going to do to the landing" to "I wonder if we can get back home again".'

The moon missions have done nothing to change human nature. They have simply confirmed that, within a detached and carefully insulated area of physical activity, emotion can temporarily be all but suspended, just so long as the capacity to predict and control events remains unimpaired. But once this capacity breaks down and the unpredictable does occur, astronauts experience emotion just as any other human being would. And when they return to earth and enter again into the life of ordinary social relationships they are probably just as susceptible to emotion as the next man. We need not fear therefore that by teaching children more efficient adaptive resources we shall cause them to outgrow emotion. Even if their practical education were of the quality of the astronauts', they would realize sooner or later that there is more to life than mere efficiency of adjustment. Where behaviour involves relationships with other people it is held that adjustment should be in accordance with what is 'right', rather than with what is merely correct or expedient, and the question of what is 'right' behaviour is one which involves complex ethical and socio-cultural considerations.

Most of what has so far been said in this chapter relates primarily (although not entirely) to aroused emotion. But what can the teacher do about recurring emotion – the emotion linked with some persistent attitude or disposition, which normally does not betray itself until critical circumstances force it to the surface? If not called forth directly in this way, it may remain hidden from the teacher's awareness. How do you deal with an emotional intensity the presence of which you cannot even recognize? This difficulty lies at the very heart of the problem as to how emotion should be 'educated', and it permits of no easy or clear-cut solution. Yet some effort must be made to resolve it, since the emotions which arise in connection with a person's basic attitudes to life usually have far deeper significance than any incidental arousal he experiences.

Fortunately, recurring emotion does not always need to be formally 'dealt with', for besides attaching to undesirable attitudes and prejudices, it attaches also to those dispositions and sentiments which we would want children to develop. An emotional attitude, I suggested earlier, is an enduring tendency to react emotionally whenever a particular object or situation presents itself, and each onset of the emotion facilitates the experience and expression of emotion, with the result that the emotional attitude becomes more deep-rooted. In the case of the person who develops an irrational fear of spiders or witches the emotional attitude is an impediment to him, which he could well do without, but not all emotional attitudes are of this type. Some are considered to be highly desirable. A person's sentiments toward his wife, his family, his home, or his intimate friends all embrace emotion of this kind, since they relate to objects which have enduring value for that person and to which he is bound by strong ties of affection. He reacts emotionally to these objects in a variety of ways, according to the ever-changing circumstances in which they happen to be viewed, but the point is that they frequently arouse emotion of one sort or another. As Magda Arnold (1960) observes: 'When someone we love is with us, we may express our affection in word and action; when he is absent, we write to him or think of him; when he is ill, we care for him, when he is lost to us, we grieve for him. All these actions and emotions are motivated and activated by our love' (vol. I, p. 199). If we are honest with ourselves, we should have to admit that we don't love another person all the time but only some of the time. Our children, whom we love, sometimes make life difficult for us, exasperating and exhausting us in ways that only those who have had children can know. Yet, throughout everything, a basic core of love for them endures, and the occasional moments when they demonstrate their affection for us, making us feel dewy-eyed and choked up inside, more than make up for the bad moments. This is the sense in which love and emotional dispositions endure. Equally enduring are some of the sentiments which relate to abstract objects – to some cause or ideal to which we are deeply committed, a virtue, a value, a religious belief, a loyalty or allegiance, an abiding interest in poetry, music, social welfare work, and the like. Even sentiments like enmity and hatred may in some circumstances be regarded as praiseworthy, as, for example, when they have as their objects tyranny, cruelty or social injustice, which all 'right-minded' people join in whole-heartedly condemning.

Far from wishing to interfere with such sentiments, the teacher may want to go out of his way to encourage them. For the past fifty years, in fact, English teachers have tended to look upon the development of desirable sentiments as one of their principal aims in affective education, although without always having any very clear idea as to how to achieve it. The unease, particularly of those concerned with education in the 1930s at this situation, was well summarized by Margaret Phillips:

'Such being the nature and importance of sentiments, what is at present known as to the laws governing their formation? Singularly little which can be translated into terms of educational policy and practice ... as regards the vast majority of sentiments into which the emotions and attitudes of the common man are in fact built we find ourselves faced with one of the biggest gaps in educational psychology' (p. 19).

Unfortunately, there has been little improvement in this

situation since Margaret Phillips' time, for we still know
next to nothing about how to develop desirable sentiments.
Contemporary educationists are inclined to turn, more in
hope perhaps than in certainty, to the vicarious experience
of reading good books as the best means of achieving it. In
Bantock's words (1967, p. 79), contact with great literature
encourages 'healthy, ethically desirable states of feeling'.
Jeffreys (1962) advocates the reading of biographical material
on more or less similar grounds:

> 'We can set before them the inspiring examples of people
> who, in all kinds of ways, found something more worth-
> while than their own comfort and safety – who lost them-
> selves to find their true selves. Example is worth a great
> deal more than precept, and biography offers an almost
> unlimited range of example. The great adventures of the
> human spirit are the heritage of our children, and they have
> a right to enter into it. We can show them explorers, like
> Nansen or Edward Wilson; scientists, like Faraday or the
> Curies; fighters, like Douglas Bader or Richard Hillary;
> workers   to   relieve   human   suffering,   like   Florence
> Nightingale, Kagawa, or Gladys Aylward. In presenting
> the lives of heroic characters, we should avoid the mis-
> take of idealizing them. Their common humanity with
> ourselves is important. What they have done we might be
> able to do' (p. 138).

The hope underlying these approaches is that, by placing
inspiring values before children, they may be tempted to
accept and assimilate them. The Plowden Report comments:
'As children listen to stories, as they take down the books
from the library shelves, they may, as Graham Greene suggests in *The Lost Childhood,* be choosing their future and the
values that will dominate it' (para. 595). They may be, but,
as with so much else in affective education as it stands at
the present time, one cannot be sure. One simply goes on
hoping.

Only when emotion is linked with the sort of pig-headed,

G

unreasoning prejudice which is damaging to the needs and interests of other people will the teacher feel justified in seeking to eliminate it. The kind of attitude, for example, which prompts skinheads to go in for 'Paki-bashing', is something any responsible teacher will want to try to change or eradicate. This type of attitude is usually based on mistaken assumptions (such as that Pakistanis are dirty, inferior parasites); it often arises from vexation, jealousy or fear (the interlopers being regarded as threats to the individual's own way of life); but its worst feature is that it forces the Pakistani into the skinhead's own stereotyped way of looking at the world, whether this pattern fits or not, refusing to recognize him as a real person who has ordinary human feelings like anyone else. Such an emotional attitude must somehow be counteracted for, as Jeffreys reminds us, whatever else changes in morality, the ground of all morality is, and always will be, respect of person for person. It *must* be one of our main objectives in affective education therefore to teach youngsters to have respect and consideration for the feelings of others.

It follows from this that the teacher should himself set an example in showing consideration and concern for the feelings of his pupils. He must be patient with their groping, tolerant of their brashness, and cherish their right to think things out for themselves. There will be occasions doubtless when, exchanging the pedagogue's hat for that of the counsellor, he will think it right to put his own cards on the table, disclosing his personal opinions on matters of moment (older children have the right to expect this much of him) but he will not wish to indoctrinate his pupils, nor impose his own moral views upon them, nor mould 'correct' adult responses for which they are not ready. Recognizing that the same truth seldom presents itself identically to the endless variety of human minds, he will forego any claim to be a moral expert with an infallible intuition of what is correct in all circumstances. He will not exploit his power to bring group pressure to bear upon deviant individual judgements. He will not want his pupils to choose their opinions, like their clothes, according to the prevailing fashion of the moment. On an important issue like racial integration there will always be conflicting opinions and attitudes and, while some of these may seem misguided, mistaken or irrational, not all of them will necessarily be prejudiced or vindictive. They may arise from good intentions and motives, and seem perfectly reasonable to their proponents. This is the crux of the problem where emotional attitudes are concerned for, as G. K. Chesterton once remarked: 'The real trouble with this world of ours is not that it is an unreasonable one. The trouble is that it is nearly reasonable, but not quite.' It is a normal and not unhealthy state of affairs for there to be differences of viewpoint on matters of social concern, and the value of publicly discussing different opinions is not simply that this draws attention to relevant facts relating to the matter in hand, but that it also obliges us to weigh our own standpoint against the observed emotional reactions of other people. This helps us to clarify our own feelings and, according to John Wilson (1967), the dispassionate examination of one's own feelings and attitudes constitutes the very essence of moral education:

> 'No question of *choosing what to do* arises until we have a reasonably clear set of desires and reactions: and by the time this stage is reached, an expert can in principle choose for us. The process of "choosing what to do" in morality, like the process of choosing what picture to buy in aesthetics, can in a loose sense be said to include an examination of our own feelings and desires: but the essential part of the process is not choice but this examination itself. Hence the essence of moral education is not the inculcation of right choices, but the improvement and clarification of feeling' (p. 65).

In seeking to educate emotional attitudes, in other words, we are concerned not so much with bringing a pupil round to a 'correct' view of what is right, as with encouraging him, after taking due account of all available information, to examine his own general feelings and dispositions as objectively as possible. We are as much interested in what he feels, as in what he thinks.

In discussing 'dispositions and feelings' Wilson (p. 60) raises the case of a mother who is cruel or indifferent to her children, without actually beating or starving them. It might be difficult to pin down specific pieces of her behaviour as immoral, but we should nevertheless say 'She doesn't love them': and we might feel strongly about this and consider that it does harm to the children. In criticizing her we would be criticizing her however not for what she did, but for what she felt (or did not feel). We would accuse her of failing to show affection, of being not disposed in the right way towards her children. What can the educationist do then to influence or modify these basic dispositions and attitudes, bearing in mind that they are usually deeply entrenched and that a person does not normally abandon them except with considerable difficulty?

Clearly, this is a matter which must be handled sympathetically and sensitively, so that the pupil is not made to feel foolish or ridiculous. Earlier, I raised the question: 'How do you deal with an emotional intensity the presence of which you cannot detect so long as it lies dormant?' In fact, latent emotion tends to rise very readily to the surface when its possessor is placed in a situation where his habitual dispositions and convictions are threatened or endangered. In such circumstances a pupil is apt to become sullen and resentful, to make sarcastic insinuations and hostile criticisms of the lesson, to resist the teacher and to blame him for his own psychological unease. Conversely, he shows satisfaction and pleasure if the teacher or the majority of his classmates appear to agree with him, thereby reinforcing and enhancing his own sentiments.

The teacher's aim in dealing with intransigent attitudes and prejudices is always that their possessor should, by comparing these for himself against the attitudes of others, modify or relinquish them voluntarily, not be coerced into jettisoning them. Indeed, coercion may be counter-productive and have the effect only of making him cling to them the more obstinately, to preserve his own system of values and self-image. (More will be said in the next chapter about the importance of the self image.) It is noticeable, for instance, that people rarely give ground on their emotional attitudes in public confrontations, no matter how untenable their position, for far too much is at stake in terms of personal self-esteem. They cannot be forcibly argued out of their convictions. This is the tragi-comic theme of Ibsen's play, *The Wild Duck*, and it goes some way towards explaining why attempts to break down racial prejudice by rational persuasion often result in failure. Instead of removing existing prejudices, attempts at persuasion appear sometimes to reinforce them. You cannot compel a person to give up his emotional prejudices: you can only create a situation and atmosphere in which he may be disposed to relinquish them himself.

While the problem of modifying undesirable attitudes and dispositions must not be underrated, the teacher has one advantage at least over the parent in that he can provide a fresh context, freed from the emotional associations of the home, in which new attitudes can emerge and take shape. The school is, or should be, a place where children can test out their immature opinions and attitudes in safety, using the teacher's and other children's emotional reactions as validating data. If the classroom atmosphere is one of experimental discovery, the pupil is protected from any far-reaching consequences of his acts, and he can thus experiment with confidence, trying on different attitudes 'for size', in the knowledge that he is not 'playing for keeps' (Kelly, 1963, pp. 162-3). The teacher should not be too anxious to correct or supply right answers to the child who is genuinely experimenting. Sometimes the validating data are more effective if they come from other children's emotional reactions.

If a teacher is willing to allow children to talk out an issue among themselves and, resisting the temptation to direct the discussion himself, is prepared to listen attentively, he may be agreeably surprised by how much children will reveal of themselves in even the most seemingly aimless discussion. In *Language, the Learner and the School* (1969) James Britton provides transcripts of discussions by sixteen-year old girls talking about their homes, which he recorded in school. The amount of implicit emotion revealed in these free-ranging talk-sessions is remarkable. In a skilful analysis of two of these discussions, one carried out with a teacher present and one with the girls left to themselves, Britton illustrates how children can help one another to deal with their emotional problems, and the manner in which a perceptive teacher can assist in this process

Drama lessons offer another excellent means of influencing emotional attitudes. Through drama a child can enter into situations which he would not normally come across, and in doing so he can begin to perceive the complexity of human situations and the endless variety of emotional responses. One of the great merits of role-playing is that, as well as encouraging a pupil to explore other people's attitudes, it enables him, under the safe protection of a mask or adopted persona, to try out his own attitudes and feelings in safety. Here again, the teacher can never know the full impact which the activity is having upon any individual pupil, although, if he follows up the drama lesson with informal discussion, pointers will usually emerge. He can encourage children to talk about what they felt while they were acting and, in the calmer atmosphere of the classroom, invite them to comment upon and evaluate their dramatic resolutions of human situations. Was that the only possible resolution? Was that how they would have wanted the situation to work out in real life?

Unfortunately, as the Report on *Drama in Education* by the Department of Education and Science (November, 1968) comments, educational drama appears as yet to have no clearly definable discipline nor generally agreed aims. It is claimed, for instance, that it has a 'liberating' effect on young people by providing therapeutic release for 'unwanted' emotion, and that by giving outlet to such feelings it can reduce the incidence of anti-social behaviour. Accordingly, it is not uncommon to find drama specialists engineering scenes of crowd violence and group conflict in the drama lesson, scenes which frequently degenerate into physical scuffles and brawls. This is only play-acting, admittedly, the dramatic convention having provided a structure whereby the experience has been isolated and distanced from real life, but one cannot help wondering whether such activities do not serve sometimes to harden rather than to weaken undesirable emotional attitudes. By all means let pupils experiment with crude, violent behaviour, in order that they can see where this leads, but when they have done with improvising and acting on impulse, let them then reflect upon the social and ethical implications of their actions.

The notion that affective education is chiefly a matter of providing 'outlet' for unwanted emotion is one which (as will be suggested in Chapter 8) is perhaps overdue for reappraisal. We certainly wish to relieve children of unnecessary emotional stress but, as I have indicated, this entails improving their cognitions and skills rather than merely encouraging them to let off emotional steam. It entails looking at those basic dispositions, values and attitudes which are prompting the unwanted emotion: otherwise one is merely relieving the symptoms rather than tackling the root problem. Emotion symptomatizes a child's basic dispositions and orientation to life, and it is only by weighing his own emotional attitudes against those of other people that he can begin to clarify them and find out where he stands in relation to others. Hence, it is clarification rather than release of emotion with which affective education should be chiefly concerned.

# 5 Social relationships

From the age of twelve to eighteen months a child is content to play at his mother's side, clinging to her for comfort and affection, and often showing anxiety when she leaves him. Then, gradually, his social disposition and range of interests extend outwards and he begins to welcome other companionship. At first, exploratory behaviour alternates with comfort-seeking behaviour, but the natural course of development is towards increasing independence of and separation from the mother, so that by the age of three a child's play is already becoming more social in direction. The first major step in the process of separation is taken usually when he leaves home to go to the play-group or infant school, an event which causes emotional disturbance if the child is not ready to part from his mother. Having once made the break and become familiarized with his new surroundings, he becomes less dependent on her and more ready to associate with strangers. His parents continue to be the main reference figures in his life, those he imitates and chiefly looks to for acceptance and satisfaction, but from the age of about six onwards he begins to move increasingly into social 'peer' groups, composed of children of roughly the same age and maturity. These are usually single-sex groupings, which favour the growth of his sex-role identity. The seven- to eight-year old boy often hates sitting next to a girl in school, and already he has the idea that dancing and kissing are feminine activities which are an affront to his male dignity. In this peer group he has to learn to play and live with others and to become accepted for what he is outside the close relationship of the family.

Then comes the onset of puberty, the effects of which continue through adolescence with important consequences for the emotions. Since infancy the child has slowly been discovering his personal identity, finding out what kind of person he is and is going to be. Until now, he has accepted his dependent status and tried to pattern himself upon his parents. His father has been his model for sex-role identification, and parental attitudes and standards of behaviour have tended to be accepted unquestioningly. But, with the arrival of puberty, glandular pressures develop as a new factor in the complex of tensions compelling the adolescent to seek out a new sex-role, and desires and longings are awakened which may conflict with earlier taboos, causing embarrassment or guilt. He begins to feel a nagging curiosity about sex and a compulsion to experiment – urges which run counter to the pattern of his previous upbringing. So strong are these feelings that he may resent his parents' authority over him and feel the need to discover a new social role and identity.

In groping to find this identity he tries out a variety of roles: cynic, man of the world, ascetic, romantic idealist, rebel and leader of lost causes (Spock, 1969). Although he still looks youthful, he considers himself to be thoroughly grown up. At thirteen or fourteen he idolizes footballers, pop stars and racing-car drivers, and is scornful of anything he regards as 'kids' stuff'. He may spend his money on trinkets for his girl friend, flaunt cigarettes openly, swear, and even boast about his anti-social activities. Girls of the same age, while still child-like in some respects, are usually more physically mature and more pseudo-sophisticated than the boys. They are obsessed with dress and their physical appearance, they use make-up freely, and often have boy-friends two or three years older than themselves. They deeply resent being 'told off' in class, or having to take orders of the schoolmarmish 'put that away' or 'look this way' variety.

As he struggles to emancipate himself from his parents' influence, the adolescent tends to lean heavily upon the ties he is forming with friends of his own age, in whose company he finds compensation and solace. He is delighted to discover that their thoughts and feelings are similar to his own, which gives him a pleasing sense of belonging, to offset the feeling of loneliness which he frequently experiences. As a mark of his apartness from his parents' generation, he may cultivate an appearance and style of behaviour which are as different as possible from theirs and which he knows, and indeed hopes, will exasperate them. As a sixth former puts it:

'He grew his hair long because it looked untidy and because he liked it that way. The rows at home didn't change his mind, in fact they almost pleased him, as did the old women who stared at him as he walked down the street, and pointed making critical comments. He was normally a shy boy, but behind that ruffled mop of brown hair which blew in his eyes and hung over his collar, he was strangely confident. Sometimes he would even give them a wink or a wolf-whistle to make their tongues wag even more.

Sam was a normal teenager with likes and dislikes and his mother couldn't understand why her nice quiet boy should suddenly become a real trouble – not that he ever did anything actually wrong; it was just the atmosphere that surrounded him, the attitude of mind that was epitomised by the unkempt long hair. Threats, bribes, arguments, nothing could make him have his hair cut; nobody could understand him.

. . . Nobody can begin to understand the turmoil in my mind. All my life I've been told what to do and where to go. Now I've decided that I'm going my way. I have a great respect for my parents and don't want to let them down but they must realise that a new me is undergoing a metamorphosis and will break out as a different person with ideas, principles and moral values that will be mine. If I form opinions that are not those of the world, those opinions are precious and I will not deny them for the whim of somebody who was just the springboard from which I will go to higher things. Already I have one principle – that I will not cut my hair. Already people notice me and I watch the world from my retreat and pass judgement unclouded by trivialities. I will not have my hair cut because here I make my stand and because I like it this way.'

Interestingly enough, the writer of this passage is a girl. The boy it describes is represented as still respecting his parents and having no wish to hurt them but, because he thinks that they neither sympathize with nor understand the 'turmoil' in his mind, he is critical of them. He relieves himself of the duty to conform to their wishes by pointing out their own moral shortcomings – their use of threats and bribes, their lack of sensitivity, the rows they create in the home. Not all adolescents express this degree of hostility toward their parents, of course, and the nature of the emotional conflict varies widely from person to person. Sometimes the strain is greatest in families where the ties are unusually strong, and where the upbringing has been affectionate but very strict. A love-orientated discipline, which uses persuasion and the threat of withdrawal of love, often results in strong guilt feelings in the recipient, whereas punitive control, which employs physical punishment and gives no reasons for its authority, tends to favour aggression, especially in boys. Whatever its causes, the point is that some degree of conflict in adolescence is both healthy and inevitable. In evolving his separate identity, the youngster is obliged to detach himself from the close protection and influence of his parents, although it is a process which inevitably causes pain.

If a child had to rely entirely on first-hand experience and his parents' communicated experience for the acquisition of all his knowledge and skills, his intellectual development and capacity to control events would proceed slowly. Socialization obliges him to modify his behaviour in accordance with the expectations of more than one group of people. By acting as he conceives other people do, he comes to understand their actions, motives and feelings better, and at the same time he learns things which he could not learn from his parents. The fact that knowledge and feelings can be communicated and to some extent shared in this way binds human beings together and forms the very basis of friendship, social life and civilization. It makes possible the transmission of culture, and it facilitates the dissemination of ideas, values and codes of moral behaviour.

Yet, as we have seen, while it is a relatively simple matter, after appropriate experience, to predict the outcome of events in the physical world, it is often difficult to anticipate how other people will behave. The 'facts' are much harder to discern in social situations and the very presence of other people influences one's appraisal of the situation and intensifies the emotional response to it. Thus, in playing with other children the three-year old discovers that they can obstruct as well as facilitate his purposes. He is frustrated not because the toy fails to work, but because some other child has stopped it from working, and the result is a fierce, tempestuous quarrel in which one child may threaten to 'kill' the other. The child also discovers that whereas in the one-to-one relationship with his mother there is only one set of expectations to be complied with, in a group there may be several. This is confusing, and it remains a recurrent problem throughout childhood and adolescence, especially for European children. As Margaret Mead (1928) observed, Samoan children, at the time she was writing, did not have to face this dilemma of having to choose among many different and mutually exclusive sets of expectations. Because they had a clearly defined role as adolescents, a well-trodden path lay ahead of them, and they were seldom confronted by ethical complexities or questions of personal choice. But the English child discovers that the parent, the teacher and the peer-group each require different, sometimes mutually incompatible, roles of him. During adolescence, the pop culture, commercial advertisers, the Youth Employment Officer, the Church and organizations like VSO or the Outward Bound Movement all appear to hold out conflicting sets of expectations.

Since social situations are often fraught with unpleasant

emotion it might be expected that individuals would avoid them more than they do. Yet to do so would be abnormal and neurotic, and contrary to the basic social disposition which exists in all of us. In any case we gain much more than we lose from social intercourse. That paradox in our nature which makes us both wish to live at ease in our physical surroundings and yet go out of our way to welcome risk and stimulation is paralleled in our social lives. We like to feel at ease in familiar company, especially when we are very young or very old, and we also enjoy meeting strangers and making new acquaintances. We alternate between the need for security and the desire for adventurousness; between dependency on what is safe and familiar, and the desire to explore and embrace what is novel and strange. If we turn back for a moment to Jonathan's essay (see pp. 12–14 above) we see what emotional arousal a thirteen-year old can experience while experimenting with social relationships. His responses might conveniently be classified as follows:

*Physical discomfort:*

'. . . the place was packed out, with hardly room to move. The mixture of intense heat and thick cigarette smoke stifled me. . . .
I put one [hand] in my pocket, but it sweated so much I soon had to take it out. . . .
I felt unwell physically: the combination of heat, smoke, piercing noise, and actually smoking two cigarettes was beginning to take effect on me. I decided to go for a short walk in the fresh air.

*Social unease:*

Naturally I was nervous at the thought of meeting other people in such new surroundings. . . .
I certainly did not want to dance until the hall was more crowded, if I danced at all. . . .
I lit one, and immediately felt more like the majority of the people there. . . .

I began to dance very self-consciously, trying to make every movement of the dance look how I would have liked it to look. . . .
All the confidence that I had gathered, all my hopes came crashing to the ground. I turned around, struck dumb, my eyes watering slightly. I stumbled to the edge of the dance floor. . . .
Strangely enough, the episode with that other girl had rid me of any nervousness that I might have had, and I no longer felt ill.'

It is crude and artificial of course to segregate physical and social responses in this way, since in emotion they intermingle indistinguishably, but by isolating Jonathan's responses to the social elements in the situation we can see how he seeks to construe 'correct' responses to events by observing and imitating the behaviour of other people. Since they have more experience of the dance-hall situation than he, he tends to accept their way of looking at things. He has a dread of appearing odd or unconventional, and he seeks ways of minimizing his incompatibilities with others – by lighting a cigarette for the first time in his life, and by 'trying to be as friendly as possible' with everyone. And yet he plucks up courage to ask a stranger to dance with him and he risks an embarrassing refusal in inviting her to walk outside. He does not always opt in other words for the safe anonymity of the crowd. When alternative courses of action suggest themselves to him he chooses in the fashion which best enhances his expectations at any given moment.

On the face of it Jonathan's behaviour is inconsistent and contradictory. On the one hand he seeks to reduce emotional arousal, yet some stronger motivating force operates here which causes him to act in ways which intensify emotion. This motivating force is the desire to enhance his self-esteem, and it relates to what is known as the 'self-concept'. There is a good deal of controversy as to the source whence this particular motive derives its energy: whether it is an 'acquired' motive, superimposed upon basic biological motives, or whether the need to actualize, maintain and enhance the self is one of the organism's basic, primary motives (Rogers, 1951). There is also controversy as to precisely what the 'self' is, although modern writers like Lewin, Cattell, Stagner and Jersild all see it as something which exists as an inner, relatively permanent structure, integrating and giving consistency and stability to the personality. According to Perkins (1958), the self-concept includes 'those perceptions, beliefs, feelings, attitudes and values which the individual views as part or characteristic of himself'; for Beatty (1969) it is 'an organization of images which each person has about himself in the world'.

We need not enter here into the controversy surrounding the nature of the self-concept. What is abundantly plain is that, whatever its origin, the desire to protect and enhance the self-image, through winning the acceptance and approval of others, is one of the most powerful of human motives and perhaps the most potent of all causes of emotion. We see its effects in the jealousies and rivalries of childhood, in the emotional behaviour of adults, and in almost every social activity that goes on in the school. As Jersild (1952) observes:

> 'There is a continuous impact between the self and the flow of experiences involved in the process of living and learning.... The learner perceives, interprets, accepts, resists or rejects what he meets at school in the light of the self system he has within him. In the healthy course of the development of the self, one is involved in a continuing process of assimilation and integration of new experiences, new discoveries concerning one's resources, one's limitations, and one's relations with oneself and with others' (p. 14).

And yet, although a great deal has been written about the relationship between the self-concept and learning processes, surprisingly little has been written about its connection with emotional behaviour.

The child's image of himself is powerfully determined by what he construes other people (especially his parents) think of him. According to Staines (1958), the child's immature self-image tends to be confused because it contains three levels of self which sometimes conflict with and rival each other. These are: (1) the cognized or known self; (2) the other self, which is based on the child's view of how he thinks others regard him; and (3) the ideal self, which is the self he would like to possess. (Other psychologists use different models to explain the development of the self: Beatty, for example, speaking of it in terms of a striving of the individual's 'perceived self' to become more like his 'picture of an adequate self'.) Such 'models of the mind' are useful, provided we recognize that they are *only* models or hypothetical constructs. Confronted with the fluid mass of grey, porridge-like matter which makes up the brain, all such models are in one sense curiously unreal. Nevertheless, Staines' model in particular does enable us to describe and to some extent interpret aspects of the child's emotional behaviour which are otherwise difficult to explain.

In most cases it is only after the child starts school, and encounters standards of measurement and evaluation other than those administered by his parents, that his self-concept can be effectively compared with those of others, and his relative inadequacies (or superior excellencies) be brought home to him in a way that was not previously possible. Emotional repercussions may then ensue. The parents may have formed an unrealistic idea of their child's ability, and refuse either to acknowledge his limitations or to be discouraged by his persistent failure at school. This puts pressure upon the child who, unable to match up to his parents' expectations, may experience feelings of anxiety or shame. Or an inadequate 'other self' may intervene. He may lower his aspiration level to that of the dullest group of children in the class and find compensation in a less demanding self-image. 'I like people who like me and resemble me' may then become his operative formula. He may go out of his way to reject those who are not like him, and perhaps be rejected by them in turn. Or, again, a child may act too much in accordance with his teacher's expectations of him, and become what Payne and Farquhar (1962) call a 'looking-glass self'.

In these instances we perceive a tendency in the child to conform with whatever expectations he feels he can best live up to, and his confusion when faced with conflicting sets of expectations. Failure to win the desired approval of parents, teacher or peer group causes anxiety, in compensation for which there may be a retreat from reality into a fantasy world, where personal difficulties can be magically resolved by processes of wish-fulfilment. The piece of writing by 'Julie', the fat thirteen-year old girl (quoted on pp. 6–7 above), illustrates this tendency well. Because her class-mates make fun of her, Julie represents them as shallow and cruel. To attract sympathy she tries to explain away her obesity – 'It wasn't because she ate a lot it was because she had weak glands.' She indulges in self-pity – 'poor old Julie' – and finally she takes refuge in improbable fantasy by winning a race against all her class-mates. These manoeuvres are a means both of arousing the reader's pity and of bolstering her own wounded self-esteem. Children often use tears for the same purpose.

Instead of facing up to the truth about herself and trying to correct the dissonance between her real self and her ideal image, Julie uses defence mechanisms as a shield. What she needs is to be guided to a truer concept of herself by being encouraged to come to terms with the person she is, instead of pursuing, through fantasy, an unattainable ideal image. She should learn to accept her limitations and make a more realistic appraisal of what her potentialities will allow her to do and what they won't. In this way she might discover excellencies in herself – a sense of humour perhaps, qualities of considerateness, patience or loyalty – which other children lack, and she could then form a more accurate appraisal of where she stood in relation to others. Meanwhile she gets no nearer to resolving her problem by resorting to fantasy.

Sometimes the retreat into fantasy is quite deliberate as

H

in the case of this fourteen-year old girl who, because her associates disparage her serious inclinations, withdraws from the world into the privacy of her own thoughts. Although still immature, in the sense that she opts out from reality rather than facing it, this girl, one imagines, will eventually develop a distinctive individuality of her own:

'It's dark and the air is dry and warm. My face looks strange in the half light. The flickering flames wriggle like snakes and disappear, gone into the soft blackness, their reflections caressing the mirror's silvered edge. And I look into it – different because I'm alone.

The book lies open on the table – it's a sad story; sad and warm – like tonight. I have read it once but I love to wrap myself in it; it shields me from the cold world.

The records are quiet, slow, sad. I'm a sad person; I love sad things. I escape into my own sad little world. It's harmless – until your mind is your world and your imagination becomes reality. Then it's the most dangerous thing on earth.

I live in two worlds. The world of my school lessons, the people who teach me, and the world of my own mind where there is a Disneyland of my own – colourful, deep. People of my own age don't understand my world; it's peaceful. Everyone's equal – no black, no white, no rich, poor, hungry, unhappy, tortured. They tell me I shouldn't bother about war, colour, death, religion – that I'm too young. I should bother about discos, boys, new clothes, records, being young and happy, but I didn't want my mind to be like this – I want to be young and carefree, but I'm old and serious. I care. So will they; but not yet.

They don't seem to get miserable and cry and feel so desperately unhappy – hating a future of O levels and loneliness. They can always find something to look forward to, even if it's only going to the disco to see their latest heartthrob. I know they're young but so am I. Why don't our minds work the same? Why can't I fall in love with a

different boy every week and laugh it off as they do? Why
do I want the same person every day for so long I can't
remember? So I don't blame them for not understanding
me – I don't understand myself.
There's one thing I do know. By the time they get old and
serious I'll have got used to it and I won't mind any more.
Because we can't all be the same. I've got my own little
mind, my own little world ... and I'm happy there ...
sadly happy....'

To the mature adult it is sometimes amusing to observe how
seriously adolescents take themselves and their problems, as
in this effusion of a sixth-form girl, upon whom the weight
of seventeen years' experience lies like the weight of untold
centuries:

> It is night;
> Dark –
> So dark
> As I lie on my bed
> Trying to sleep.
> I hear a young child
> Crying –
> Shattering the calm
> And my thoughts.
> That child knows nothing of problems;
> It cannot understand life.
> But I know –
> I am learning.
> The middle-aged cry – overwhelmed;
> The old cry – unable to remember;
> And I cry,
> For I know too well how problems
> Shape my young life.

It is tempting, as I say, to dismiss such writing as immature and affected, and to want to reassure the adolescent
that this crisis through which she is passing is only a tempor-

ary, intermediate phase. Yet to dismiss it is to risk losing her
confidence and to be insensitive to the very real emotional
problems she is facing. What Loukes (1965, p. 111) says of the
best approach to religious education applies equally here:
namely, that the ground for discussion should preferably be
the ground on which the adolescent himself stands. 'We
must take seriously what he has learnt about life, what he
feels about it, what he has to say about it: we must take
*him* seriously.' This is not to say, of course, that the teacher
should not, at some point, express a judgement, even a critical
one, upon the things adolescents say to him (a point to which
I shall return).

I have indicated how the child's lack of a strong sense of
personal identity tends to make him uncertain and awkward
in social situations, and vulnerable to emotion whenever his
self-image is threatened. But what about the grown-up, for
whom this crisis of personal identity, as Erikson (1968) terms
it, is presumably past? Is he any less susceptible to emotion
in his personal relationships? The fact is that, while the adult
has probably developed a stronger self-image than the adolescent, he feels the same need to maintain and enhance it and,
consequently, anything which threatens this image is apt to
cause emotional upset. He likes to feel secure among the
people he lives and works with, and, unless he is very sure
of himself, he dislikes intensely the feeling of being the odd
man out in a group. Some experiments by Asch (1955) and
Crutchfield (1955, 1962) bear interestingly upon this matter
and throw additional light on the nature of emotion.

Asch found that most adults experience emotional stress
if their opinions are found to be at variance with those of
other people in close face-to-face proximity with them.
Because of the confusion and embarrassment such a situation
creates, some people will agree with almost any opinion put
forward by the rest of the group, no matter how preposter-
ous it is, provided the group endorses it unanimously. Asch
contrived his experiment in such a way that all the members

of the group, apart from the individual being tested, were 'confederates' of the experimenter, instructed beforehand to give unanimously *false* judgements on test-items like: 'Which of these three lines is longest?' 'Which shape is larger?' (items in which the correct answer was unmistakable to any person who was not being thus pressurized). The person being tested was invariably placed near the end of a row of people, so that he gave his judgement following most of the group and thus his judgements, if honest and correct, were always in opposition to the false answers given unanimously by the pre-arranged majority.

'Candid' photographs filmed during these experiments (plate 2), together with testimonies supplied afterwards by the subjects who took part in them, indicate the degree of emotional disturbance most people experience when they find their judgement on clear-cut perceptual or logical problems at variance with the judgement of a group of other people. Asch comments:

'Most subjects miss the feeling of being at one with the group. In addition, there is frequent reference to the concern they feel that they might appear strange and absurd to the majority. One of the strongest [independent, non-yielding] subjects reported: "Despite everything there was a lurking fear that in some way I did not understand I might be wrong; fear of exposing myself as inferior in some way. It is more pleasant if one is really in agreement." Another subject asserted: "I don't deny that at times I had the feeling to heck with it, I'll go along with the rest." Or "I felt awfully funny, everything was going against me." "I felt disturbed, puzzled, separated, like an outcast from the rest. Every time I disagreed I was beginning to wonder if I wasn't beginning to look funny" ' (see Crutchfield, 1962, p. 509).

Crutchfield's subjects in an analogous experiment reported similar emotional symptoms. Some began to doubt their own mental competence and felt dejected, isolated or anxious.

They could not 'make sense' of the discrepancy between their own judgements and those of the group. Bogdonoff (1961) took physiological measurements of the increase in plasma-free fatty acid level – an index of central nervous system arousal – and found that the fatty acid level remained high in those subjects who resisted the group pressure, but was reduced among those who yielded, suggesting that the act of conforming resulted in a lowering of emotional arousal.

The results of Asch's and Crutchfield's experiments give some cause for concern. If, merely to relieve emotional pressure, people yield to opinions which at bottom they know to be false, then it seems that at heart they are conformists, not autonomous individuals, since their desire to avoid social embarrassment overrules all other considerations. Yet faced with the blunt choice whether we would prefer children to grow up to be independently minded or conformist, parents and teachers would surely opt unhesitatingly for the former. We think it right that children should take into account the opinions and attitudes of others, but we hope that ultimately they will develop minds of their own and not conform to other people's views merely because their own feelings are being pressurized. One recalls, in this connection, A. S. Neill's (1962) indictment of the English state school – that it produces a moulded, conditioned, repressed type of child. '. . . He sits at a dull desk in a dull school; and later, he sits at a duller desk in an office or on a factory bench. He is docile, prone to authority, fearful of criticism, and almost fanatical in his desire to be normal, conventional, and correct. He accepts what he has been taught almost without correction . . .' (p. 95). No one wants to produce children of this type: children who, as future citizens will be dominated by mass opinion and turn their backs on every issue which upsets them. We want them to voice their opinions freely, and to be capable of withstanding emotional pressures if, after due consideration of all the factors involved, they remain convinced that their private opinion is correct.

However, it is possible to place quite a different interpretation upon the results of Asch's and Crutchfield's experiments (as Crutchfield himself has done), and one which bears significantly upon the work of the teacher. Firstly, it must be remembered that the subjects of these investigations had been accustomed from birth to construing other people's behaviour as a means of shaping their own behaviour, on the assumption that they, like themselves, were seeking correct responses to events. Secondly, they were also accustomed (albeit unconsciously) to recognizing emotional agitation as a signal whenever their interpretations of events were incorrect. When in this experimental situation therefore emotion flashes warnings to the individual that his seemingly sound judgements are suddenly and inexplicably going astray, he is totally disconcerted. He *knows* that shape A is larger than shape B, and yet four other people, equally capable of judging (whom he doesn't realize have conspired to mislead him), declare that B is larger than A. He is trying to get the right answer but, as Crutchfield (1962, p. 521) observes, he 'assumes that each other group member is trying equally hard to get the right answer'. In this situation he may be tempted to ascribe greater validity to the group judgement than his own.

Crutchfield found that when subjects were given 'feedback' information, confirming that their judgements were correct, their confidence was immediately bolstered and thereafter they remained more independent of the group. They also tended to hold firmly to their own opinions in tests involving judgements of aesthetic taste, an area in which it is commonly thought that one person's opinion is as good as another's. Conformity was always greatest where the individual was least sure of his ground: for example, where the objects to be judged were highly complex or ambiguous, or ones on which other members of the group were thought to have expert qualifications for making judgements.

These results are scarcely surprising. If in real life we are unsure about matters on which important decisions are called for, we don't usually make wild, on the spot judgements: the sensible course is to take steps to acquire fuller information in order that our judgement can be checked against relevant facts. This is more or less what happens, or should happen, in school. The pupil should be given access to 'feedback' information and validating data by which to check his ideas and opinions. In the complexity of modern life however we cannot ascertain at first hand the relevant facts about every object we come across, and it is convenient and sometimes prudent to avail ourselves of the judgement of some recognized expert – the doctor, the electrician, the lawyer (a tendency which is widely exploited by commercial advertisements of the 'doctors recommend', 'our experts say' variety). When a pupil finds that the correct answer is not readily forthcoming he expects the teacher, by virtue of his expert knowledge and authority on his subject, to provide the right answer. We should not be afraid therefore of supplying information on matters on which we are experts. Children sometimes want to be told things rather than struggle to discover these for themselves, knowing all the time that the teacher has a short cut to the right answer. Yet the prestige and power of the teacher's position place a heavy responsibility upon him, for there is a double sense in which he represents authority over the immature minds in his charge. He is not only *an* authority, by virtue of his specialized knowledge, but also *in* authority, as the person delegated to preserve order in the classroom (Peters, 1966, p. 240). It is this second source of his authority which places the teacher in such a strong position to manipulate group pressures in the classroom. He can utilize these pressures either to enhance or detract from pupils' images of themselves, and to minimize or intensify emotional stress.

The aim must be of course to shield children from exposure to intolerable group pressures and to protect them from the consequences of any mistakes they happen to make while trying out and experimenting with opinions and attitudes. Emotion will arise soon enough of its own accord when a child finds that he cannot get the right answer to a problem which is troubling him. There is no point in exacerbating the emotion by adding to it the pressure of adverse group opinion,

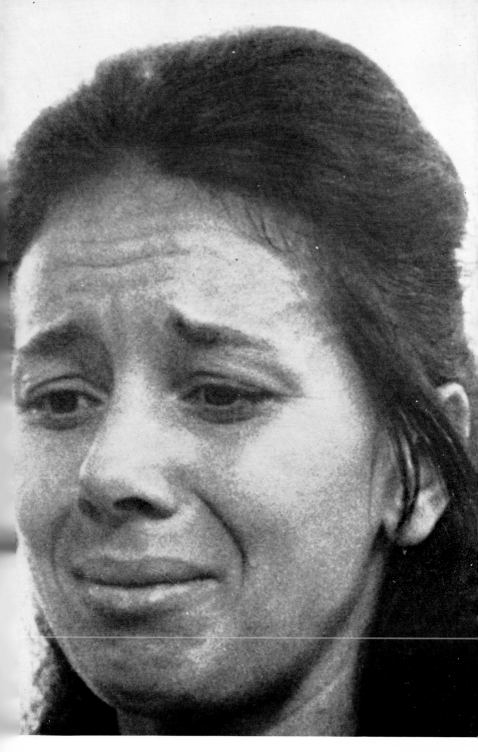

What emotion is she feeling? (See page 188 below)

A session in progress during Asch's social pressure experiments in the Laboratory of Social Relations at Harvard University. Seven subjects are asked by the experimenter (*right*) to compare the length of three lines, or to say which of two shapes is larger. Six of the subjects have been coached beforehand to give unanimously wrong answers. The seventh (*sixth from left*) has merely been told that it is an experiment in perception.

Some emotional reactions at Wimbledon, June 1970.

Child audience reaction to a puppet-show.

as will happen if a child is made to feel inferior or different from the rest of the class, or if the teacher is foolish enough to ridicule the child who gets the wrong answer. What basically the child wants of the school is the opportunity for forming and testing his opinions, dispositions and attitudes without fear of embarrassment. The ratio of unpleasant arousal will decrease to the extent that the validating procedures are made objective, impersonal and devoid of all threat to the self-image.

The teacher who is aware of the emotional complexities inherent in all group situations, and of the threats which these pose to the child's image of himself, will take steps either to counteract them or to turn them to useful account. Oeser's book, *Teacher, Pupil and Task* (1955), contains a simple introduction to the ways in which sociometric procedures may be employed in the classroom to protect children's social and emotional susceptibilities. The teacher should also be careful about the chance comments he throws out in class, comments which the pupil may interpret as positive or negative reflections upon himself. Staines (1958) has shown that teachers' casual, unpremeditated comments have a more adverse effect upon pupils' personal images of themselves than is generally realized, and that the character and frequency of these may, cumulatively, have a marked influence upon individual children's progress and attainment. Marie's self-image is flattered if she is selected for the part of Cinderella because she 'has the best complexion in the class', and Jack will feel equally pleased if the teacher says 'Jack, you're tall. Help me with this', but the effect of these comments on those who are not chosen is open to question.

Earlier, I mentioned discussion and improvised drama as useful means by which children can compare their feelings and attitudes with those of other people. They can also explore human relationships without risk to themselves through the vicarious experience of reading books, listening to radio, and watching television or films. Vicarious experience keeps the child safely distanced from situations which in real life might be painful, and it has the added advantage that it can be terminated by simply turning a knob or laying the book aside. Through these media the child's range of experience is extended: he can observe how other human beings behave in situations which he himself has never encountered and, by processes of empathy and identification, he can, as it were, enter into their feelings and problems. The mechanisms by which the processes of empathy and identification operate, and the reasons why we can feel sympathy for the lot of a stranger, are not as yet fully understood. Whether sympathy for another person is based upon our own sense of insecurity (the remembered experience of total helplessness which we suffered as infants) or upon the contrast with our present state of well-being, it is difficult to say. What is certain is that children do identify with characters presented to them in stories, films and the like (see pp. 7–8 above). You have only to observe a child listening to *The Ugly Duckling* or watching *Dr Who* to know that this is so (see plate 3).

In an investigation which bears interestingly on this matter Lenrow (1965) devised an experimental situation in which thirty-three American children, aged from three to five years, were seated individually at a table before a small puppet theatre. In a preliminary session the puppet was introduced to each child as a real creature rather than as a puppet, and the puppet and the child played a simple game together, after which the puppet gave the child a present, because it had been 'such fun' playing with him. After a short interval, the puppet then reappeared in a scene representing a forest. He wanted to get home, but his way was blocked by a barrier which he could not move by his own efforts (it was a piece of cordwood, which projected out from the stage and across the table towards the child). The puppet expressed distress because he could not move the log and appealed for help. He was beset by other difficulties, too: the need to pick up some twigs which lay just beyond his reach, and to procure a gift similar to the one which he had previously given the child.

in order to appease a witch who was menacing him. The results of the experiment showed that of the 33 children, 13 helped the puppet to overcome a physical barrier (8 giving help before being asked to do so directly), a majority gave verbal support and encouragement, and only 7 children made no attempt to help the puppet. The experiment raises a number of problems that need to be investigated further, but it certainly indicates how fully some children do enter into the imagined feeling of others.

Reading about other people's experience or observing it being enacted in the cinema or theatre not only helps to clarify our own amorphous feelings and attitudes, but it also tends to unite us with others in a common humanity. To witness emotion unfold in a televised real-life drama, as during the ill-fated Apollo 13 moon mission, is to become conscious that other people are sharing simultaneously in feelings similar to one's own. This capacity for shared feelings which human beings possess is one which we prize and would not wish to lose, even supposing that it could be eradicated, which seems unlikely. Admittedly, contagious emotion can be dangerous if it leads to mass panic or mob violence, but it can also be harmless, and even agreeable and uplifting. The effect produced by some of Churchill's wartime speeches on English listeners is a case in point. On a humbler level, crowd reactions to notable occasions in sport can also be poignant and emotionally satisfying. Our hearts go out to the player or athlete who is fighting an uphill battle against some crippling handicap – injury, loss of form, unfair conditions, or some younger, more powerful opponent. David Gray, a *Guardian* journalist, describing Gonzales' epic victory over Charlie Pasarell in the 1969 Wimbledon tournament, conveys vividly what it felt like to be on the Centre Court that day:

'After the longest singles contest ever played at Wimbledon, the old man had triumphed in one of the finest and most emotional matches on the Centre Court since the war.

Pancho Gonzales, aged 41, and former champion of the world but never of Wimbledon, beat time, weariness, and expectation in defeating Charlie Pasarell, the best first-day player in the tournament, as both Santana and Rosewall remember, 22–24, 1–6, 16–14, 6–3, 11–9....
It was a match that cannot be discussed in ordinary lawn tennis terms. Here was Gonzales, gaunt and greying, the great player, fighting desperately. On Tuesday night, complaining bitterly about being forced to play on in semi-darkness, he had been booed by sections of the crowd. Yesterday, there was only cheering. Pasarell, younger and stronger, challenged him all the way, and reached match point seven times. Gonzales was so tired that he could scarcely hold his racket, but he saved himself – twice from 0–40 – and went on to win the match. It was the kind of match that took your breath away, and moved you to tears at the same time....
In the end he had to win. Any other result would have been emotionally wrong.'

One can think of many similar such occasions in sport which (to adopt a phrase of Scott Fitzgerald's) have started the cymbals crashing and plucked the strings of innumerable nervous violins: Ron Clarke, for instance, struggling against the effects of altitude in Mexico City; Stanley Matthews at long last winning a cup-final medal; Gordon Richards winning his one and only Derby; Bobby Charlton, Matt Busby and Manchester United winning the European Cup; Herb Elliott at the Rome Olympics; Beamon's breath-taking long jump; Christine Truman, or almost any woman tennis-player you care to mention, competing against a top-ranking American. In witnessing such spectacles, whether they are scenes of triumph or disappointment, crowds are not only bound closer together by emotion, but they actually *use* their emotions – by cheering, shouting, stamping and so forth – to indicate to their favourite that they are on his side and feeling for him. By their expression of emotion they will him to still greater efforts (see plate 4).

The emotions aroused in social situations can be pleasant or unpleasant, desirable or undesirable, exhilarating or frightening. And yet, as we have seen, emotion is always secondary to and dependent upon the motives, dispositions and cognitions which prompt it. It so dominates some situations that we are apt to forget this. For some obscure reason, which we don't bother to analyse, we want Gonzales to win today, although yesterday we booed him. His winning has become a matter of such concern that every fluctuation in his fortunes sends a flurry of emotion around the tennis court. His victory matters more for the moment than anything else, even at the risk of hurting Charlie Pasarell's feelings! (Well, we need not lose any sleep over this, for Charlie is probably used to the fickleness of tennis supporters.) This is the sense in which sport provides an outlet for feeling, in that it takes people's minds off other things, and provides a simple, clear-cut situation in which many individuals can share simultaneously in the same emotional experience – a rare occurrence in everyday life. We need not feel ashamed of such emotions, nor bother to analyse them too closely. As a character in Noel Coward's play, *The Vortex*, remarks: 'It's fun analysing one's emotions, but we can't be analysing them all the time, for it kills sentiment stone dead'.

Nor can the teacher be analysing emotion all the time, although it behoves him to keep a constant finger on the pulse of the class and to be sensitive to sudden fluctuations in emotional temperature. Situations can develop almost without warning, if the teacher is inexperienced or new to the class, when emotional contagion can spread like wildfire. It is as though the whole class were spontaneously moved by a common desire to find out how far they can go with this new teacher (Morrison and McIntyre, 1969, p. 110). On the

face of it, their lawless behaviour looks like a deliberate
flouting of authority, but it is really the pupils' means of
testing out the security of the school. It is as if the pupil is
saying 'I hope you can hold me' not 'You can't hold me!'
(Ashwell, 1962). A student teacher tells of a class who began
a sit-down strike in one of her lessons. They sat on top of
their desks and refused to budge. But having done that, they
did not know what to do next. They felt ridiculous and baffled
for, as one of them afterwards confessed: 'We do not enjoy
misbehaving, but something drives us on. We push and push
just to see how far we can go until a teacher stops us.' They
are like birds trapped in a cage and longing to be free. Yet,
once free, they have no idea where to fly.

It is for this reason that the teacher needs to keep a
grip on the reins, and not be afraid to indicate his disapproval
of undesirable attitudes and behaviour. To do so is not to
be authoritarian in the pejorative sense of that word, but
rather to earn the gratitude and relief of the pupils. They
feel the urge to kick over the traces occasionally, and yet
they need the security of knowing that someone is there
ready to take control of the reins again and guide their
actions. Above all they need teachers who maintain consistently firm standards (especially in schools where they meet
many different teachers). The teacher who tells a pupil in a
kindly but firm manner that in this particular instance he is
wrong or behaving badly is doing him a service, and indicating
at the same time that he is genuinely concerned about his
welfare. Where pupils do not sense this unsentimental care
and concern for them, they feel an inarticulate sense of
bewilderment and resentment.

We owe it to adolescents, as they struggle to make sense
of the world and their place in it, to give them firm guidance
and standards of behaviour. Instead of being exasperated or
giving way to their excesses, we need to remind ourselves
that these are their ways of testing our reactions and finding
out where the 'lines' are to be drawn. They want to know at
what point we will stop them. Any teacher with experience of

unruly classes knows this to be true. Beneath the bravado and surface rebelliousness, adolescents are desperately unsure of themselves. Not only do they lack a strong sense of personal identity and a clearly defined role in the frame of things, but they are scared of the mysterious biological changes, especially the bewildering sexual upheavals, which are taking place inside them. As samples of their writing quoted in this chapter have shown, they recognize acutely the insecurity, the seeming aimlessness and 'unreality' of their lives. They want to become adults and to form deep and personally satisfying relationships, especially with members of the opposite sex. But they are inexpert at construing other people's behaviour and, boys particularly, find it difficult to communicate their feelings tenderly, with the result that they often appear confused, awkward and gauche.

To help adolescents overcome their emotional problems requires tact, forbearance and sympathetic understanding. The teacher must shield them from intolerable group pressures while they try out new attitudes and ideas, and, as Loukes says, he must take them and their feelings about life seriously. Without attempting to mould them or impregnate them with his own ideas, he must be ready, when called upon, to put his own cards on the table and to indicate plainly what he thinks is good behaviour or a reasonable point of view. At the same time he must be prepared on occasion to have his own views and attitudes challenged. By these methods education becomes a two-way process, in which the pupils will sometimes educate the teacher, helping him to bridge the generation gap and to revise his own attitudes and dispositions where these need modifying or revising.

# 6 How do we recognize emotion?

I remarked earlier that emotion has a valuable signalling function, in that it enables an infant to express his needs to his mother and it also provides information which may indicate to a teacher what course of action is appropriate for dealing with a particular pupil. Through emotion we communicate something about ourselves to others, and by interpreting other people's emotional signals we learn something about them. But how precisely do we recognize emotion in another person, especially if he is trying to conceal it, as people often do? Does emotional sensitivity require some special power of empathy – some mysterious 'third ear', as it is sometimes called – or can it be developed by experience and training? In this chapter I shall consider some of the instruments used for detecting emotion, also the various non-verbal signals by means of which animals and human beings communicate emotional meaning. Finally, the question will be raised whether the ability to discriminate and interpret children's emotional signals can be improved by systematic training.

As we have seen, it is sometimes difficult to interpret the emotional reactions of people who are strangers to us – people riding on a roundabout, for instance. Unless they choose to describe their feelings for us, we can know little about them, nor about the internal bodily changes they are experiencing, since these are hidden from our eyes. Yet it is possible, with the aid of what are commonly called 'lie-detectors', to monitor some of the bodily changes which occur in emotion – changes in brain-frequencies, eye-pupil dilation, respiration, heart rate, psychogalvanic reflex, and so forth.

Until recently, much of the apparatus used for this purpose was cumbersome and fearsome-looking, enough to frighten the subject by its very appearance. Today, there are inconspicuous, 'socially acceptable' monitoring devices available which can conveniently be carried about on the person, so that the subject can go about his everyday business, or pursue a whole range of outdoor activities (including riding on a roundabout) while the instrument transmits information about his bodily changes to observers stationed some distance away. These instruments mark a breakthrough in the field of neuro-physiological research. They enable us to investigate emotional responses in 'real-life' situations, removed from the intimidating atmosphere of the clinical laboratory.

Electrocardiographic equipment has been used, for example, to measure the heartbeats of a trained parachutist while he was actually falling through the air towards earth. From the time of his leaving the aeroplane to the anxious moment immediately before the parachute opened his heart rate was found to accelerate from 95 to 185 beats per minute (Hughes, 1966). It has been used, too, to measure the heart rates of experienced racing-car drivers during competitive motor-racing. In the *British Medical Journal* (18 February 1967) Taggart and Gibbons report that in some cases drivers recorded 200 to 205 heartbeats per minute just before the race started. It was used to measure the heart rates of the original moon astronauts on lift-off, the reported rates being: Armstrong 110, Collins 99 and Aldrin 88, figures significantly less than on their Gemini flights, when they were respectively 146, 125 and 118. These last sets of figures indicate, incidentally, how emotional stress tends to lessen as confidence grows from repetition of experience.

With the aid of electrocardiographic equipment we could (conceivably) measure and compare different children's emotional reactions, or observe the progressive decline in a child's stress-level as he learnt, by developing skill, to cope with some difficult challenge. But this is to assume that heart rate increase necessarily signifies emotion. Unfortunately, it

I

does not. I can, after all, increase my heart rate merely by the physical effort of bending down to pick up a book, and even while I am sitting perfectly still in a chair irregularities of heartbeat pattern may occur quite unpredictably, as the result of a phenomenon known as sinus arrhythmia. Heartbeat recorders, in short, cannot distinguish reliably between those effects which are due mainly to physical exertion and those due to increased attention: the investigator has to infer a difference from his knowledge of the stimulating situation.

Moreover, these monitoring instruments can detect only those emotions which are accompanied by marked sympathetic arousal. They cannot differentiate between two physiologically similar, yet subjectively different, emotions like anger and fear, nor can they tell us anything about a whole range of other emotions, such as sadness, sympathy and nostalgia, which involve mainly parasympathetic activity and which, although less violent, may be equally 'moving'. Recently, I monitored an eight-year old boy's heart rate while he watched children's television films like *Tarzan*, *Casey Jones*, and *Dr Who*, and found that, while he watched film sequences involving pathos, his heart rate remained constant somewhere near his normal base line of 70, in sharp contrast to what happened during more exciting sequences when it sometimes accelerated beyond 100. Yet, watching the boy closely and talking to him afterwards, one could not doubt that he was as much moved by these sad sequences, although in a different way, as he was by the more violent episodes. It is parasympathetic activity however which brings the lump to our throats and the tears to our eyes and, unfortunately, there is no means of measuring these phenomena, for tears, unlike raindrops or heartbeats, are not a commodity which lend themselves to scientific quantification.

To explore a person's subjective experience instruments like projection tests, attitude tests, mood-scales, questionnaires and personal interviews are commonly used, these being sometimes followed up by psychoanalysis. The projection test presents the subject with certain situations (in pictorial, symbolic or verbal form) and invites him to interpret these in any manner he pleases. The theory is that by allowing him to apply his imagination freely he may unconsciously project his own emotional attitudes into the situation. By discovering patterns of significance in ink-blots, by interpreting pictures which tell a story or by the completion of unfinished sentences, he may reveal something of the workings of his innermost mind. It is claimed, for instance, that the degree to which a person is self-centred, or concerned for the feelings of others, can be inferred from his performance on the Rorschach coloured ink-blot test. Free-composition drawings and paintings are thought to reveal something of their creator's emotional 'set' towards the world. According to H. A. Murray (1943), persons writing stories in response to Thematic Apperception Test pictures reveal all kinds of emotionally-coloured motives which they would not otherwise own up to – motives like self-abasement, deference, exhibitionism, aggression, a desire to dominate, to achieve, to win the affection of other people and so forth.

But how a subject draws a picture, construes an ink-blot, or tells a story, depends not only upon emotional factors but also upon his artistic or linguistic capabilities, which may or may not enable him to express effectively what he feels. How the investigator interprets a subject's performance on a projection test depends to some extent moreover upon *his* personality and understanding. There is no guarantee, for example, that the pictorial or verbal symbols employed mean the same thing for both subject and investigator. How one interprets a projection test performance is a highly subjective matter therefore, and it is not surprising to find that clinicians frequently disagree among themselves in interpreting the results of these tests. (In an attempt to bridge this gap a device called the semantic differential has been invented by Osgood and his associates at Illinois University, designed for the measurement and analysis of meaning itself. Osgood *et al.*, 1957.) There is likewise disagreement or uncertainty very often about the results of questionnaires or personal interviews designed to explore a person's subjectivity, since subjects do not always answer questions truthfully, or they take exception to the way a question is put or to the personality of the interviewer, or they give what they think is the socially 'correct' answer or the answer which the investigator wants them to give.

In fact most of the instruments which we possess at present for measuring or identifying aroused emotion or emotional attitudes are limited or deficient in one respect or another, although they are undoubtedly useful provided their short-comings are recognized and accepted. Plainly, the majority of them could not be used in the classroom, except by turning the school into a psychological laboratory. Hence, the teacher must fall back on other, less sophisticated, means of detecting emotion in children. The most obvious means open to him is the traditional method by which human beings and animals have always recognized emotion in one another – namely, by attentive observation of facial expressions, bodily movements and changes of vocal tone.

Whether animals do in fact experience emotion in the way that human beings do we can only speculate since, while it may be doubted whether their emotional experience is any-thing like so complex as ours, strictly speaking, there is no means of knowing what animals feel. A farmer's wife, Linda Moller, writing in the *Guardian* recently, suggested that farm animals are capable of experiencing anxiety or bereavement as intensely as human beings do. She described how newly-weaned lambs, when parted from their mothers at three months, craned their heads in the direction of the ewes and 'cried'. '. . . They cried all through the night: and in the morning their voices had grown hoarse and deep, like those of children who have cried too long. Throughout the next day they stood there still looking in the same direction, by now exhausted, and their cry reduced to an occasional bleat.' She described also how 'a poor horse was desperate for company' and how, on the day calves are taken from the cows to be sold, no one in the vicinity reckons to sleep much that night. 'The cows bellow their anxiety for the best part of a day and a night, and have on occasion bent and twisted a heavy iron gate in their efforts to break through and go and search for their calves.' There is however no way of comparing the intensity of animal emotions and those of humans in similar circumstances. What we *can* say with confidence, and without resorting to anthropomorphism, is that the signalling codes which animals use to evoke corresponding responses from other animals certainly resemble human expressions of emotion.

Animal signals are always conspicuous and usually quite unambiguous. Thus, baring of teeth, bristling and growling, as well as being autonomic means of preparing for attack or defence, signify a clear warning to others, meaning: 'Keep away, I am hungry', or 'If you encroach upon my territory, I shall attack you' (Cullen, 1967). Sometimes, these threatening gestures are highly ritualized, as when two apes make ready to fight. 'The contestants circle one another in a characteristically stilted fashion, their bodies tense and stiff. They may bow, nod, shake, shiver, swing rhythmically from side to side, or make repeated short, stylized runs. They paw the ground, arch their backs, or lower their heads' (Morris, 1967, p. 154). When an animal expresses friendliness these hostility signals are more or less reversed. In the case of a dog, muscular rigidity, bristling hair and growling are replaced by fluid relaxation, a wagging tail, a smoothing of the hair and an ingratiating whine. Apes express friendliness by physical embraces, by forms of greeting like lip-smacking, and by gentle stroking or grooming.

These animal signals facilitate social communication much as human emotional expressions do. They provide information about the animal's present state of functioning ('I am hungry', 'I am sick'), and they evoke corresponding responses in other creatures. In higher species like apes and monkeys which, it is said (Van Hooff, 1967), can register as many as thirteen different facial expressions, the range and variety of these signals is considerable. Indeed, animal codes are in some respects more expressive than ours for, although less open-ended or flexible, they are also less inhibited. As children grow up, they learn to control their features to a certain extent and to restrain gestures which are considered socially improper. They acquire speech which, while it facilitates communication, also enables them to disguise their emotions to some extent.

Fortunately for the primary school teacher, young children are not usually adept at concealing their emotions. They vent these openly where an adult might restrain himself or merely smile politely. Yet, by the age of nine, a child is already learning to lower his eyes and blush. Faced with some awkward social contretemps he will sometimes cover his confusion by hiding his face in his hands, for he knows that his face can give him away. He tries consciously to hold back his tears and 'keep' face. These inhibitions derive from the socio-cultural ethos in which he is brought up. In England a boy soon discovers that there is a taboo upon intimate self-presentation. He finds that he is expected to repress feelings which are considered 'effeminate'. (Similarly, Chinese girls are instructed not to smile readily nor to show their teeth when they smile.) The development of such internalized restraints makes it increasingly difficult for the teacher to penetrate the child's defences.

The words a child uses to describe himself moreover are often intentionally misleading. 'I am not frightened', he says, although he looks white-faced and trembling, and there is a perceptible quaver in his voice. Or he says 'Yes' with such obvious reluctance as virtually to signify 'No'. The words used are a contradiction, in short, of what he is actually feeling. However, the non-verbal signals which accompany his speech – changes in facial expression, vocal tone and bodily posture – are indications of emotion which are much harder to control. Speech is mediated by specialized areas of the higher central nervous system, permitting of a high degree of conscious control, whereas non-verbal modes of expression are governed by autonomic, lower levels of the nervous system which are much more instinctive. Facial expression is the most important of these non-verbal modes for, although less spontaneous and less intense than other non-verbal signals, it is much more specific. Facial expression, it is true, often retains a certain element of ambiguity – surprise can easily be mistaken for joy or fear, contempt can be confused with disgust (Schlosberg, 1941) – nevertheless, it is to another person's eyes and face that we normally look first for indications of emotion.

The main messages signalled by the face are, probably: joy, sorrow, pity, fear, anger, hatred, disgust, contempt, relief, interest or boredom, impatience, anxiety, frustration, pain, surprise, shame and amusement. These messages are signalled by changes within the facial configuration – eye movements, eyelid positions, eyebrow and mouth positions, and sometimes by a rush of blood to or from the skin surface. The wide range of cues by means of which the face can register its different signals is conveniently classified for us in Kendon and Ex's *Notation for Facial Postures* (1965).

*A. Eyes*

Under this aspect the modes are distinguished in terms of the way the lids are disposed around the eyes. The modes are as follows:

1.   Normal, or baseline position. Eyes open, lids relaxed.

2.   Half-closed. Upper lid falling relaxedly over the eyeball.

3.   'Tight eyes'. Upper lid drawn forwards over eyeball, lower lid tightened, drawn upwards.

4.   'Screwed eyes'. Both lids drawn tightly together usually with accompanying contraction of zygomatic musculature.

5.   'Laughing eyes'. Eyes narrowed or closed by contraction of zygomatic and levator musculature, but eyelids relaxed.

6. ⟩      'Frowning eyes'. Eyebrows lowered over eyes, partially closing them.

7. ○      'Widened eyes'. Both lids drawn back from eyeball.

### B. Brows (including forehead)

1. ら      Normal, or baseline position.

2. ⌒⌒      Raised brows.

3. ⟋⟍      Sloping brows. The brows are drawn upwards and together.

4. W      Knitted brows. The brows are drawn together over the nose as in a frown.

5 ⪡      The brows are drawn downwards over the nose, with transverse wrinkling above nose bridge.

### C. Mouth

1. ⎯⎯      Normal or inexpressive mouth.

2. ⎯θ⎯      Normal or inexpressive mouth, open.

3. ⌣ ⌣      Mouth with slight smile at corners.

4. ⌣      Smiling mouth.

5. ᵕθᵕ      Smiling, mouth open.

6. ⩔      Smiling mouth, lips parted to expose teeth.

7. ᵕθᵕ      Smiling mouth, open, lips drawn back to expose teeth.

8. t⎯t      Mouth with corners slightly tightened.

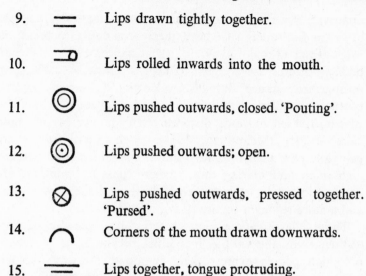

9.     Lips drawn tightly together.

10.     Lips rolled inwards into the mouth.

11.     Lips pushed outwards, closed. 'Pouting'.

12.     Lips pushed outwards; open.

13.     Lips pushed outwards, pressed together. 'Pursed'.

14.     Corners of the mouth drawn downwards.

15.     Lips together, tongue protruding.

16.     Lower lips protruding. 'Half pout'.

The bodily postures by which affective messages can be conveyed – position of head, shoulders and trunk, positions of hands, arms and legs – likewise admit of considerable variety (although it has not proved possible as yet to evolve a satisfactory notation for hand and arm movements).

Animal signals, as we have seen, are often highly conventionalized. So, too, are some of the more basic human signals. Raised eyebrows, for example, are generally seen as denoting surprise, half-raised brows as worry, a single raised eyebrow as disbelief, wide-open eyes as alertness, half-closed eyes as boredom, an up-curved mouth as happiness, a down-curved mouth as distress (Harrison, 1965). Certain hand movements too are fairly universal. An involuntary hand-to-nose movement often signifies fear, fist gestures – aggression, fingers to lips – shame, an open hand dangling between the legs – frustration, forehead wiping – tiredness, face rubbing – reassurance (Krout, 1954a, 1954b; Ekman and Friesen, 1967). Similarly, head nodding or shaking imply approval or disapproval; lowering or raising of the head implies submission or a bid for superiority; head turning, a desire to break off eye contact (Argyle, 1969, p. 104; Chance, 1962). Different bodily postures are adopted to express liking or dislike – an open-armed stance implies welcome, an arms akimbo position, coupled with avoidance of eye contact and the placing oneself at some distance from another person, indicates dislike (Mehrabian, 1968). High-arousal states are generally expressed by a fast rate of speech, by loud volume, high pitch and blaring timbre; more 'passive' emotions are communicated by slower speech, lower volume, lower pitch and a more resonant timbre (Davitz, 1964, p. 185).

These classifications are helpful but too broad for distinguishing the various individual permutations by means of which people express their emotions, for everyone has his own way of expressing joy, anger or sorrow. Wide-open eyes, for instance, signify not only alertness but also threat or a challenge for dominance, while half-closed eyes betoken anxiety or amusement as well as boredom. Similarly (depending on the context of the action) head-lowering sometimes implies belligerence, not submission. Some non-verbal signals moreover carry quite different meanings in different cultures. The action of sticking out the tongue is a good example. In parts of China it signifies an apology, in parts of India – the evil eye, in Tibet – deference, whereas in England it is a rude sign used by children. Hissing is used in Japan to show deference to superiors; in England it is a way of expressing disdain (Argyle, 1969, p 86). Even within a particular culture the fashion in these matters changes periodically. For example, now that English football crowds are becoming familiarized with Continental manners, they are as likely to whistle at opponents as to boo them. It would be fruitless therefore, as Argyle points out, to try to compile some kind of dictionary by which to translate non-verbal signals into specific, recognizable emotions, since the same emotion is expressed differently by different people, and at different times.

Attempts have been made in the past to improve a person's

skill in identifying emotion by inviting him to concentrate on one particular non-verbal signal at a time – a procedure which has led to some curiously artificial experiments. Subjects have been asked, for example, to interpret emotion by looking at faces depicted on still-life photographs, drawings, or identikit faces, or from listening to actors reciting the alphabet in tones of voice intended to simulate different emotions. Actors have been presented with 'affectively neutral' sentences like the following: 'I am going out now. I won't be back all afternoon. If anyone calls just tell them I am not here' – and have been required to recite these sentences in such a way that a tone of admiration, affection, amusement, anger, boredom, despair, disgust, fear, impatience, joy, love or worship, predominates. Then subjects have been asked to identify these different emotions from tape-recordings (Beldock, 1964). It is of course quite impossible to infuse a tone of admiration or worship into such sentences, as anyone who doubts may try for himself. Even professional actors have found the task beyond them and, not surprisingly, most such experiments have yielded mediocre results. A face frozen into immobility by the camera lens conveys little information unless we know the circumstances in which the photograph was taken. A disembodied voice is able to simulate emotion plausibly only within the context of an appropriate situation – a radio drama, for instance, or in the reading of a poem.

In real life no one would ever think of interpreting emotion by considering facial expression or vocal tone in isolation from the rest of a person's demeanour. Each separate signal is only part of a total pattern of responses and we are accustomed to looking for supplementary cues – bodily posture, movements of the hands, the actual position a person takes up in relation to someone else – to facilitate identification. Thus, in anger, we may detect flushing, frowning, clenching of the fists and teeth, a rise in the pitch and intensity of the voice. Fear is perhaps identified by blenching and sweating, by a drooping at the corners of the mouth, starting of the eyeballs, rigidity, a thin, high-pitched voice. In joy there is relaxation and smiling, and sometimes even tears. To interpret and identify emotion accurately, a complex interpretation of several interrelated cues is needed therefore, also, as mentioned earlier (see pp. 56–8 above), an adequate vocabulary for differentiating the different emotions. Even then, identification is unlikely to be accurate unless one is given some knowledge of the situation which prompted the emotional reaction, for, as the very term emotional 'response' implies, emotion is a reaction to something specific.

There is little point, therefore, in studying emotional expression except in relation to the situation which causes it. In fact, one of the principal conclusions to be drawn from experimental work in this field is that, while it is easy to arrive at erroneous interpretations if expressions of emotion are considered in isolation, identification improves markedly whenever relevant situational cues are provided. If there is conflict between facial expression and situation, then those who are judging almost invariably follow the situational cues, not the signals (Fernberger, 1928). M. Sherman (1927 and 1928) asked adult subjects to identify the emotional reactions of infants in response to such things as delay of feeding, sudden loss of support, restraint of head movements and being pricked with a needle. When adults saw films of the infant reactions, without being given information about the stimulating conditions, they could not guess what had caused the reactions, nor could they agree among themselves as to what emotion was being expressed. When the presentation of these emotional reactions was preceded by *incorrect* stimuli moreover, the interpretations went wildly astray, since judges almost invariably followed the false situational cues rather than the actual signals. Thus, an infant's response to obstruction of movement was interpreted as a fear reaction because, in the film, it was seen to be preceded by an unexpected fall. When subjects were given genuine situational cues however, they usually labelled the reactions correctly.

The classroom teacher is normally in a good position to

study emotional reactions in relation to their situational contexts, but he can hardly be expected to discriminate at one and the same time the fleeting, distinctively different, emotional signals emanating simultaneously from thirty or more children, who differ widely in their past psychic experience, in their levels of development, and in the extent to which they have internalized emotional restraints. Faced with a new class particularly, he may not be able to do much more than keep his finger on the general pulse and be on the look-out for signs of unusual disturbance. Fortunately, the problems lessen as the teacher's knowledge of his pupils increases (for, as Hebb's and Köhler's studies of chimpanzees have shown, the recognition of emotional expression improves significantly as one comes to know one's subjects well). As the teacher gets to know the children's capabilities, and is able to set pupils work appropriate to their aptitudes and levels of attainment, they should seldom be called upon to operate at a level likely to induce severe emotional stress. From talking to them individually and checking regularly upon their work he comes to know them as persons, so that he can detect when an emotional response differs markedly from a child's normal base-line, or when there is a significant deviation from past performance.

Provided the teacher consistently pitches the work at a level which each child can cope with (an approach which may necessitate some use of group teaching methods or individual assignments) and provided he takes reasonable precautions to prevent any child's self-image being seriously threatened, then the incidence of emotional disturbance is likely to be rare. Only occasionally will situations develop where widespread emotionality is likely, and even these situations will often be predictable or avoidable. A lesson on sex, for example, can be expected to produce emotion, since it may come into conflict with parental taboos, and (as we saw in Chapter I) the inspection of living chick embryos in the course of the first-year Nuffield Biology Project can also arouse strong feelings. Sometimes, on the other hand, we hope that children *will* become emotionally involved in a lesson, and see no harm in their entering passionately into the feelings of others or acquiring emotionally-toned sentiments in regard to such matters as social justice, cruelty to animals, pollution of the environment, and the like. Probably there will be only a few children in each class whose emotional volatility is so unpredictable as to demand close unremitting observation. It is important therefore that the teacher should be able to identify and recognize emotion when it occurs. By being sympathetic, consoling, or helpful, he may be able to do something to relieve the emotion.

Can we do anything then to help teachers to identify children's emotional signals more accurately? Is emotional sensitivity a gift of nature or can it be developed by training? These are matters to which educationists have hitherto given little attention, with the result that those who are about to begin their teaching careers may find themselves in something of the dilemma described by this student:

'If I were setting out at this time, the beginning of my teaching career, to learn how to be sensitive, empathic, and emotionally understanding as a teacher, I would       ·· very little help in present day psychological literature.

Like most teachers I will eventually learn to behave in a way that seems relatively sensitive to the feelings of others. And gradually, as I continue teaching, the problem of how to be or to become sensitive to emotional communication will recede, and I will apparently feel that in some mysterious way I had become reasonably empathic, appropriately intuitive, and emotionally sensitive. But when it comes to telling anyone else how to be sensitive to how their pupils are feeling, then it will be difficult to be sure of the basis of my judgements on their insensitivity, although I will be sure it exists.'

Can we do anything too to make teachers more aware of their own non-verbal signals, and of the effects which these can have upon their pupils? We do not want to make teachers so hyper-selfconscious that they will fear to look a child in the eye lest they do irreparable damage to his psyche, but there is surely a case for demanding that teachers should have some awareness of how influential their own non-verbal signals can be. A recent experiment bears this out.

In an investigation carried out by Rosenthal and Jacobson (1968, pp. 160–2) in an elementary school heavily populated with 'disadvantaged children', pupils were tested with a new intelligence test unfamiliar to the teachers. The teachers were then informed in a casual manner that, 'in case they were interested', some children, who were named, had done well on the test and had achieved scores indicating that they would probably make unusual intellectual gains during the coming year. After a year the test was repeated and the results showed that these children had in fact made the gains predicted. The significant point about this experiment is that the children mentioned had not in fact done well on the test in the previous year, but had merely been chosen at random from each class. They had received no special instruction from their teachers, but had gained because their teachers had expected them to gain. The ethics of this experiment, whereby some pupils were deliberately put in an advantageous position at the expense of other children, although open to question, are not our immediate concern. All sorts of reasons could be advanced to explain the improved performance of these children, among which we should need to include the stronger motivation which resulted from enhanced self-esteem (the mirroring of the teachers' more favourable expectations). But how did the teachers communicate their higher expectations to the pupils? The experimenters concluded that these must have been communicated by subtle, non-verbal signals (reinforced doubtless by casual, self-referent comments of the sort mentioned by Staines – see p. 109 above).

Whether we heed them or not, in fact, non-verbal signals are constantly being exchanged in the classroom, conveying significant information about the attitudes and dispositions of their senders. Different postures are used to express liking or dislike, eye contacts are attempted when pupils are seeking to establish a relationship, the rate of eye blinking goes down when a person is thinking or concentrating upon something, and speech carries messages according to how it is said as well as in terms of its content. Sometimes these signals can be intrusive and irritating, especially if they merely reflect other people's signals, as when a pupil does a take-off of the teacher behind his back. Or the teacher unconsciously opens his book while beginning to speak and infuriatingly (as a student puts it) all the pupils open *their* books. He happens to mention how someone's head was chopped off, or he casually introduces a word like 'police car' or 'pig' and, instantly, if it is a junior school, spontaneous imitations of executions, wailings of police-car sirens, gruntings and holding of noses break out all over the classroom. Sometimes, conversely, it is the very absence of non-verbal interchange which is irritating. The perspiring teacher waits in vain for a response from the stolid, wooden faces before him, or, as a sixth former complains, there is 'no feeling' in his European history lessons, because they consist of solid dictation with everyone's face buried in a book.

Granted then that it is useful to a teacher to be able to discriminate and identify children's emotional signals, let us return to the question of whether this ability can be developed by training. Evidence accumulating from recent research in this field suggests that, although some people are by nature more sensitive to emotion than others, emotional sensitivity can be systematically improved if we are prepared to take trouble over it. It appears to depend not so much upon intuition or distinctive personality correlates, as upon perceptual and cognitive factors (particularly verbal intelligence) which can be developed by training (Beldoch, 1964; Davitz and Mattis, 1964). Normally, it improves steadily with age (Dimitrovsky, 1964) and it may also be related to the ability to recognize emotion in oneself (Levy, 1964). In an experiment which bears interestingly on this topic Jecker and his associates (1965) found that teachers' accuracy in judging

whether children understood what they were being taught
was greatly improved if their attention was directed, under
skilled guidance, to the children's facial expressions and
gestures.

If it were decided that all student teachers should be encouraged to develop their emotional sensitivity, what kind of
training would be appropriate? Clearly, the traditional
methods for imparting knowledge – lectures and self-instruc-
tion through reading – would have only secondary value here,
since the main emphasis would need to be on direct observation of real-life behaviour. As Argyle observes, people
cannot be taught about non-verbal behaviour by verbal
methods alone: they can learn these skills only by practising
them, just as one learns to swim by swimming, or to ride a
bicycle by actually riding a bicycle. As a preliminary, students
could be given opportunities to observe children's behaviour
on films (some of the films produced by the Tavistock
Institute of Human Relations are excellent for this purpose).
The other day, some of my own students were discussing the
film *Nine Days in a Residential Nursery* (1969), which
depicts the deterioration of John, a seventeen-months old boy,
who is separated from his mother while she has another
baby, and who is placed in a residential nursery where unfortunately he cannot secure the individual care which he
needs. The students commented freely upon the various signs
of emotional disturbance which John increasingly displays
during the course of the film, pointing out specific signals
which they thought would at home have brought his mother
running to his side, but which here were ignored, because
none of the nurses fully realized the extent of John's plight
or they were too busy to give him their undivided attention.
The following comment (taken from a tape-recording of our
follow-up discussion) indicates how deeply engrossed one of
the students became in this film, and how closely he had been
observing John's non-verbal signals:

'... In the end in fact there's little change in his facial

K

expression, it's just one of anguish all the time. It's as if he's no longer using his face, and he starts to use his arms then. When he cried on the first day, he used only his face, he was only crying – his eyebrows and things. But by the last day he was using his hands, he was thrashing about a bit – he was burying his face in his hands, he was plucking at his ears – he was doing all sorts of things. There was just a confused range of reactions going on all over the body. . . .'

There is more profit to be gained from studying films of this kind, which deal with actual, on-going behaviour, than can be derived from reading any number of books on the subject – as the authors of such books would doubtless agree. In addition to studying films, students might also be given facilities for observing child behaviour through one-way viewing screens, or by means of audio-visual recordings of actual lessons. With the aid of such devices the spontaneity of the children's actual responses could be preserved, uncontaminated by the presence of an audience. Thus, students could comment on reactions as these occurred, and they could also compare notes during play-back discussions.

With the aid of these devices it would also be possible to make students more aware of their own non-verbal signals. For instance, they could take over classes themselves occasionally, while other students observed through the one-way screen, and, if they were willing, they could have their own lessons videotaped, so that the effectiveness of their interaction with the pupils could afterwards be discussed. Neilsen (1962) found that 'self-confrontations' of this kind caused Danish students to become much more alert to the non-verbal signals they themselves transmitted, and that the experience gave them valuable new information about themselves. A further refinement would be to use an earphone through which the instructor could communicate directly with the student, drawing attention to significant cues while the lesson unfolded (Flanagan, 1961). A less sophisticated and less expensive method of directing attention to the importance of emotional cues, although one which lacks the advantage of dealing with children's responses, would be to have students acting out role-playing situations themselves, under the guidance of a tutor.

There is still the problem however that the interpretation of emotional signals is a highly subjective matter, and the likelihood consequently that observers will disagree among themselves in their interpretations, even in cases where they know the subject well and are witnesses to the actual situation eliciting the emotional response. If only, beneath the deceptively simple elements of human communication, we could discern some general laws or principles operating, we could approach this matter more objectively, instead of leaning so heavily upon subjective impression. But are there such laws? Until very recently it would have appeared that there are not, and yet now, as the result of some fascinating developments in the field of social psychology, the conviction is growing that the processes which underlie social interaction are in fact governed by certain general principles. Indeed there have already been attempts to formulate these principles.

It is claimed that if we look at a person's *total* behaviour in response to a situation, predictable patterns begin to emerge. When two people enter into conversation, for instance, the initial position they take up in relation to each other is thought to be determined by critical factors which vary according to the setting in which the conversation takes place, the degree of intimacy between the speakers, and whether there is a disposition toward co-operation or conflict. The speakers' postures likewise vary according to their respective attitudes towards each other. During the conversation facial and bodily movements provide each speaker with information about how his message is being received, and non-verbal signals convey information about his emotional state which may reinforce or (in some cases) contradict the actual words he uses. During the encounter eye contact between the speakers varies according to their spatial proximity, and according to the intimacy of the topic of conversation, the speakers' mutual relationship, and whichever person is speaking at the time. There seems to be an essential equilibrium in fact involving spatial proximity, eye contact, facial expression and intimacy of topic (Argyle and Dean, 1965):

$$
\text{Intimacy} = f \begin{cases} \text{proximity} \\ \text{eye contact} \\ \text{smiling} \\ \text{personal topics of conversation, etc.} \end{cases}
$$

If one component in this equation changes, the others thereupon tend to be readjusted, so that the balance is restored. In intimate situations involving more than two persons, similar equilibria, involving additional variables, obtain.

The above account, based upon Michael Argyle's book *Social Interaction* (1969), to which I am indebted (and which the reader is advised to consult for fuller information on this topic) suggests that there *are* laws governing the processes of social interaction, and that these processes can be studied objectively, without recourse to any mysterious power of empathy or intuition. If such is the case, then the systematic training of emotional sensitivity becomes a real possibility. It means that students can watch films and video-recordings of children's behaviour, and relate what they observe to some theoretical framework. At present, this original way of looking at social interaction lies mainly within the social psychologist's province, and its applications to the classroom situation have yet to be worked out in detail. However, the signs are that what will eventually emerge from this new field of research may enable teachers to understand the non-verbal processes at work in the classroom better than ever before. By a combination of all the methods described in the above pages it should be possible not only to alert student teachers to the importance of non-verbal signals, but to give them positive help in developing emotional sensitivity, instead of leaving them, as we do at present, to muddle along as best they can, learning these necessary skills on the job.

Yet, when all is said and done, the interpretation of emotional signals can be a highly complex matter and we need to be realistic about what we can hope to achieve in this direction. Clearly, it is going to take more than a few audio-visual sessions to improve the emotional sensitivity of the student who has not hitherto developed this capacity very greatly. We cannot simply thrust a manual of instruction into his hands and expect that he will thereupon be able to discriminate and interpret accurately every subtlety of emotional expression which human beings are capable of displaying. Merely by noting that someone's eyebrows are raised, that the eye-lids are relaxed, that there is a slight smile at the corners of the mouth, will not automatically enable him to fathom the depths of emotion implied, for example, in a situation like the following, which is a description of a meeting between Nicholas Rostóv and Sónya, taken from Tolstoy's *War and Peace.*

'When Rostóv met Sónya in the drawing-room he reddened. He did not know how to behave with her. The evening before, in the first happy moment of meeting, they had kissed each other, but today they felt it could not be done; he felt that everybody, including his mother and sisters, was looking inquiringly at him and watching to see how he would behave with her. He kissed her hand and addressed her not as *thou* but as *you – Sónya.* But their eyes met and said *thou,* and exchanged tender kisses. Her looks asked him to forgive her for having dared, by Natásha's intermediacy, to remind him of his promise, and then thanked him for his love. His looks thanked her for offering him his freedom, and told her that one way or other he would never cease to love her, for that would be impossible.

"How strange it is," said Véra, selecting a moment when all were silent, "that Sónya and Nicholas now say *you* to one another and meet like strangers."

Véra's remark was correct as her remarks always were, but

like most of her observations it made every one feel uncomfortable; not only Sónya, Nicholas and Natásha, but even the old countess who – dreading this love affair which might hinder Nicholas from making a brilliant match – blushed like a girl' (p. 323).

This is how a great novelist delineates the subtleties of emotional communication, and it is an approach which one would not wish the student to ignore. Nor is it one which is in any way superseded or invalidated by any of the methods outlined in this chapter. In alerting students to the importance of non-verbal signals, we need in fact to avail ourselves of every variety of approach which may be helpful.

Non-verbal signals are being communicated all the time in the classroom, whether we like it or not, but hitherto we have paid too little attention to them, with the result that there is more emotional muddle and indeed suffering in our schools than there need be. We talk loftily about 'educating' the emotions, and yet ignore actual symptoms of emotion which are being transmitted before our very eyes. However, there are signs at last that this situation may be changing. Already, several colleges of education are making use of one-way viewing screens, films and audio-visual equipment to direct students' attention to pupils' affective behaviour, and students are responding enthusiastically to these methods. They welcome any methods, in fact, which help to bridge the gap between theory and practice, and which provide fuller insight into children's emotions.

# 7 Language and emotion

It is difficult for adults to imagine what it is like to be an infant because we cannot recall any experiences of our own prior to the time when we had language to encode them. Our own experience is so linguistically structured that we find it almost impossible to conceive a learning process in which language plays no part, and yet, miraculously it seems, every child learns to speak his native language without having any language through which to learn it (Halliday, 1968). From the host of unfamiliar stimuli which bombard him he learns to listen attentively and to distinguish human noises from other noises. Without benefit of language he learns to decode and encode for himself a new world of sound and meaning. It is a quite remarkable achievement and one which can never be repeated.

Having language gives the child much greater freedom than animals from environmental constraints, for it enables him to express his uniquely human wants and needs effectively, and it facilitates co-operation in the face of a hostile environment. It creates new feelings and needs, which animals, whose signalling codes are more rigid and inflexible, do not even know about (Osgood, 1967). In thinking about the world and trying to make sense of his experience, in acquiring his system of beliefs, attitudes and values, and in developing his personal identity, the child relies heavily upon words, for words are a convenient device by which he is able to symbolize his thoughts, ideas and feelings. Without words he would be restricted to reasoning in the concrete, the physical and actual, and he would be unable to think effectively about absent objects or to relate present to past experience.

Language renders perception more precise and yet more generalized. By means of language the child learns to isolate a particular object from its surroundings and to mark out its essential distinguishing features. What was previously a vague shape becomes suddenly and permanently 'a cup' for drinking out of, and from this percept he advances to the concept of cup, which then serves as a yardstick by which to distinguish other objects whose function is different – 'a knife ... for cutting', 'a plate ... for eating from'. Language is thus essential to perceptual and cognitive development: as Luria puts it, the word isolates, abstracts, systematizes and generalizes.

The significance of language in cognitive development is well illustrated by Luria, in his book *Speech and the Development of Mental Processes in the Child* (1959), in which he describes an experiment with a pair of identical twins, Yura and Liosha, whose speech development was retarded (because of phonetical impairment and because, *being* twins, they were not under the same pressure that the single child is to develop speech as a means of communication). As a result of being exposed to a special language programme, Yura, originally the more retarded twin, showed a steady improvement in IQ tests and eventually outstripped his 'control' brother. Or consider the plight of the deaf-mute infant. Because he is deprived of speech this type of child is restricted to primitive, elementary thought-forms. He has difficulty in passing beyond a concrete, visual mode of thinking, and he may never master abstract, conceptual thought or fully comprehend terms like 'guilt', 'equality' or 'democracy'. The problems of trying to make sense of the world without a verbal language for translating raw experience into meaningful units are vividly described in Helen Keller's autobiography.

I am not concerned here however with the importance of language in higher intellectual activity, nor with problems of speech pathology, articulation, linguistics, phonetics, reading and spelling. My present concern is with the relationship of language to emotion. How does language structure emotional experience? To what extent can a child's internal feelings be made explicit through words? How do speech and writing differ as modes of communicating emotional meaning?

Apart from using language to acquire information and for clarifying problems which puzzle him, the infant also uses words to express feelings and desires. Lewis (1963, pp. 35–39) suggests that all the child's first words are associated with emotion or bodily needs and that only gradually does their cognitive meaning clarify. Thus, a word like 'Mama' can mean anything from 'I am hungry', 'I am uncomfortable', to 'I am happy' or 'I like doing this'. Strictly speaking, we cannot be certain that all a child's first words relate to his bodily needs for, as always, we are faced with the problem that the infant's experience can only be inferred. (A friend of mine kept a record of his son's first recognizable words and observed that at eight months he had said these words, in this order: 'car', 'daddy', 'mummy', 'more', 'clock', 'teddy', 'all gone', 'mock' [smoke], 'bird', 'yes', 'gone'; and at twelve months: 'fish', 'park', 'bowo', 'papple', 'vase', 'pretty', 'gogog' [golliwog].) Nevertheless, Lewis's theory is broadly correct: most of the first words a child uses do relate to objects associated with his family, his home and his immediate needs and desires.

When a child begins speaking – which he does largely by processes of imitation – it is not the content of speech which he tries to master and internalize, so much as the intonational and rhythmic patterns of what he hears. Since these patterns are expressive of the relations between the human participants in a situation, indicating whether one person is agreeing with the other, disagreeing, asserting, questioning or confirming, they convey a sense of the speaker's attitude or emotional 'set' toward the situation, and it is the clues to these constantly varying relationships between the speakers that the child listens for. His parents occasionally quarrel or laugh about matters which in themselves are incomprehensible to him, but, while the substance of what they talk about is meaningless, the manner in which they address one another is of the utmost significance. Similarly, it is not the logic of an argument which impresses the infant, but the status and tone of the person who is putting it. As Halliday (1968) observes: when a little child says to you *my daddy says so,* with the fall-rise tone on *daddy,* he is using the resources of English intonation to convey a great deal about his own standpoint on the matter.

A child learns how to express his feelings and emotions by observing how his mother and other people express theirs. As his world broadens and his needs become more complex he realizes that these needs are better understood if he expresses them in words, and that by using language he is more likely to secure the response he seeks. Increasingly, therefore, words take over, so that instead of merely crying for food, or banging the table with a spoon, he asks for it. Instead of expressing anger, hostility or self-assertion through physical gestures like hitting or biting, which his mother tends to frown upon, he begins to use 'hitting' words, which symbolize the same thing but are less socially reprehensible (Gardner, 1964, p. 171). More and more he finds that he is obliged to communicate verbally, whether he wants to or not, yet at the same time he finds that putting his feelings into words makes them more bearable. It is pleasant to find himself in verbal agreement with others, and to find that someone else sympathizes with and shares in his sorrows and joys.

The more language the child internalizes the better he is able to differentiate his own confused mass of feelings and to mark out clearly defined attitudes toward things. He no longer feels vague satisfaction or vague dissatisfaction, but knows that it is this particular object which elicits this particular feeling. As his emotions thus become more differentiated and precise, his awareness of himself as a person is developed. Here is yet another respect in which deaf children suffer as a result of their linguistic deprivation. Having no opportunity as infants to hear how adults express their feelings, these children remain tied to primitive expressions of emotion. Because they can neither discriminate effectively nor adequately express their feelings, they often appear moody, aggressive or emotionally unstable – as Helen Keller did, before she internalized the means of communicating with other people.

Linguistic development does not depend solely on physical well-being or maturation however, although in general it is true to say that the older we are the better equipped we are to verbalize our emotions. Social-class factors, as Bernstein (1958, 1959, 1960, 1961) has shown, are also crucial in the acquisition of language and in determining the range of emotions which can be felt or expressed. Bernstein (1959) distinguishes between two codes of language, a 'restricted' and an 'elaborated' code, which correspond roughly to working-class and middle-class usages respectively. Because the elaborated code is ampler in vocabulary, more flexible in its structures and in its capacity for making logical relationships, the elaborated-code user, Bernstein suggests, has a wider perceptual range: he 'sees' more cues inciting an emotional response. Because his code is a superior instrument for analytical thinking and for the investigation of subjective states, he is also more aware of himself as a complex being, more conscious of his motives and intentions.

The restricted code, on the other hand, tends to narrow and intensify the range of stimuli to which responses are possible. Its possessor is thus excluded from certain types of perception and may lack the ability to handle certain types of relationship. He is not interested in remote causes underlying events, but prefers the present, the actual, the 'arrived', without wondering how it came to arrive. Rather than struggle to express his feelings verbally, he prefers to transform them into immediate, unreflective action. The verbal cues which stimulate his emotions tend to be obvious and direct – the abstract, the subtle or the ambiguous making little or no impression upon him. According to Bernstein (1961) restricted-code users have fewer guilt feelings than elaborated-code users but tend to be more anxious and more liable to feelings of shame. Their self-awareness, their understanding of their own motives, is underdeveloped and hence they find it easier to dissociate themselves from their own acts and the consequences of these. If pressed for explanations of their behaviour they often become anxious or confused.

It follows from Bernstein's hypothesis that the capacity for verbalizing emotion differs markedly according to whichever linguistic code one habitually uses. An elaborated-code user, like Jonathan, whose essay I discussed earlier (see pp. 12–14 and 97–8 above), is able to describe his feelings with considerable precision. The restricted-code user is unaccustomed to analysing his emotions in this way. Among his kind 'communication goes forward against a backcloth of closely shared identifications and affective empathy, which removes the need for elaborate verbal expression.' The verbal expression of emotion, such as it is, tends to be disjointed, halting, cliché-ridden, and full of sympathetic circularity – a string of 'you knows', 'wouldn't its', and so forth, which require from the listener only a reinforcing response. It is a language of implicit rather than explicit meaning in which, according to Bernstein, it becomes progressively more difficult to make subjective intent more explicit.

Social-class factors may thus restrict the range and quality of cues which arouse emotion, and also prevent a child from differentiating clearly between his emotions. They may hinder him from expressing his emotions adequately and so make it difficult for persons outside his social group to interpret or understand his feelings. Moreover, the expression of certain tender emotions such as affection, love or grief may be drastically inhibited by the mores of the sub-culture to which the child belongs. Pressure to conform to the kind of feelings approved by the group as a whole may mean that, although the working-class child does in private experience tender emotions, he may suppress these as undesirable (or at any rate, think it undesirable that others should see them). From fear of social ostracism he may disguise his tender emotions under a veneer of toughness.

Until more follow-up research has been done on Bernstein's

theory it would be unwise to apply it categorically to any individual child's linguistic behaviour, and, in any case, as Bernstein's latest paper (1970) indicates, this whole theory is still in process of being developed. Because a child habitually uses a restricted code we should not automatically assume that he will therefore suppress certain kinds of emotion or be emotionally less stable than the elaborated code user. We would need to observe his performance in many different kinds of speech and writing situation before we could arrive at any firm conclusions about his emotional characteristics. The limited evidence afforded by Howard's short piece of writing (see pp. 11–12 above) is a case in point. For some teachers this piece, though lacking in depth or subtlety, shows an imaginative realization of a human situation and some authentic exploration of that experience. But, according to one of my former students:

> 'Howard's tender feelings are hidden by his assertion that his Mum will be "all right" – she won't be seeing men die day and night. Sad farewells are obviated by concerns about everyone getting into the car. He doesn't explore his feelings about the navy very deeply in words, giving the *impression* that he hasn't any – "Mike be good seeing atlacing all day". Perhaps he daren't betray his real emotions – perhaps they are blurred because he is unable through verbal and social restrictions to express them. He is passive rather than active, and the vagueness and latency of his feelings seem to provide consolation – almost to embody a philosophy of life with which to deal with problems.'

The difficulty of determining the degree of emotionality underlying Howard's essay is that in itself the essay provides insufficient data on which to base a decision: we simply don't know enough about Howard as a person. Despite his failure to analyse his feelings, there certainly seems to be some tender concern for his mother (a concern which might have been suppressed in an oral situation).

My student's point about the suppression of emotion

amounting almost to a philosophy of life is important. It is borne out whenever a restricted-code user who has survived some ordeal involving emotional stress is interviewed on radio or television. In such interviews it is seldom the stolid working class voice which quivers with emotion; it is more likely to be that of the interviewer (the elaborated-code user), who tends to infuse his own feelings into the situation. But what if a restricted- and an elaborated-code user were subjected to the *same* ordeal – like making a parachute jump for the first time? Conceivably, their heart-rate and general physiological responses might be similar, yet any verbal descriptions of this experience which they afterwards provided would presumably be different – one account being baldly factual perhaps, the other more 'poetic'. Theoretically, an elaborated, reflective verbalization of the experience ought to bring the emotions under better control, by structuring and refining them, and relating them more closely to previous experience. But is this what would happen – necessarily? We think of those phlegmatic restricted-code users who in wartime have endured extremities of stress to which their more articulate companions have succumbed. We think of tough little street-urchins who show better self control in certain situations than their middle-class counterparts.

Stoicism, courage and daring involve different emotions of course than those which the elaborated-code user excels at expressing, and they depend upon factors other than linguistic dexterity. They depend to some extent, for instance, upon a person's capacity for dealing with the situation confronting him, and upon his basic dispositions and attitudes to life. We need to be on our guard perhaps lest we become too preoccupied with the part played by language in the development of emotions like guilt, shame and anxiety. There are other emotions, such as those associated with qualities of heroism, fortitude and enterprise, which are no less important and whose characteristics we have hardly begun to explore. What makes one person braver than another? Why do some individuals habitually prefer fight to flight, and vice-versa?

It would be interesting to know what part speech development plays in the formation of these attitudes and in the
emotions associated with them.

As we saw in the last chapter, it is possible to communicate
purely by non-verbal means, this being the main mode
of communication between animals, and sometimes between
humans. An accomplished actor or actress can 'speak vol-
umes' without words, the very act of *not* speaking sometimes
signifying more than words could ever do. Then there is the
kind of empathy described by George Orwell at the beginning
of *Homage to Catalonia,* where he meets an Italian soldier
for the first and only time, and writes: 'It was as though his
spirit and mine had momentarily succeeded in bridging the
gulf of language and tradition and meeting in utter intimacy.'
But most of our communication is carried on through words
(reinforced in oral situations by non-verbal signals) and,
generally speaking, we find words adequate for our purposes.
    It is only when we wish to articulate emotions or elements
deep within our private consciousness that we sense the inadequacy of language, for, as T. S. Eliot observed in *Burnt
Norton:*

> . . . Words strain,
> Crack and sometimes break, under the burden,
> Under the tension, slip, slide, perish,
> Decay with imprecision, will not stay in place,
> Will not stay still. . . .

Somehow, words never fully express the feelings which we
want them to express. Thus, Mandler (1962, p. 303), discussing the difficulties of investigating the private experience of
emotion from the viewpoint of modern behaviourism, writes:
'I cannot possibly use the rather crude instrument of language
to express the myriad impressions, feelings, ideas, notions,
and emotions that flood my private screen. I can attempt to
approach it, but will forever feel frustrated in trying to do
these feelings full justice.' And even when speech is orchest-

rated with the full accompaniment of non-verbal features (gesticulation and facial expression) and extra-verbal features (intonation, stress, pace, pitch, emphasis and pauses) a speaker may still feel that it fails to convey his intended meaning. This, according to Michel Quoist (1963, p. 52), is a perpetual dilemma for the evangelizing preacher:

> I spoke, Lord, and I am furious,
> I am furious because I worked so hard with gestures and with words.
> I threw my whole self into them, and I'm afraid the essential didn't get across. . . .

It is not necessarily that one's grasp of language is deficient, but that language itself, by the laws of its very nature, is too inflexible and clumsy an instrument for communicating certain forms of subjective awareness. The logical structures and conceptual units which makes up language render it an excellent vehicle for the expression of factual statement or argument (what Susanne Langer calls 'discursive symbolization'), yet these same characteristics are a hindrance when we try to articulate inner subjective experience.

The problem is not simply shortage of vocabulary, as in the impoverished language called 'Newspeak' in George Orwell's *1984*:

> 'The purpose of Newspeak was not only to provide a medium of expression for the world-view and the mental habits proper to the devotees of Ingsoc, but to make all other modes of thought impossible. . . . To give a single example. The word *free* still existed in Newspeak, but it could only be used in such statements as "This dog is free from lice" or "This field is free from weeds". It could not be used in its old sense of "politically free" or "intellectually free", since political and intellectual freedom no longer existed even as concepts, and were therefore of necessity nameless. . . . Newspeak was designed not to extend but to *diminish* the range of thought, and this purpose was

indirectly assisted by cutting the choice of words down to a minimum' (p. 241).

Indeed, it is the very richness of the vocabulary available which is sometimes an obstacle to the communication of emotional meaning. Feleky (1922) found, for example, when he asked 100 subjects to describe the photograph of an actress seeking to express hatred through her facial expression that they used 39 different terms to label this emotion. The words most employed were ugliness (13 times), disgust (11), hatred (8), disdain (8), mockery (7), antipathy (5), repugnance (5), defiance (5). Nor is the problem that the grammatical and syntactical structure of language so determines our thought-processes as to preclude us from verbalizing our subjective experience effectively.

The problem is rather that the extent to which emotions can effectively be put into words is determined by what language is and is not capable of doing. The Newsom Report observes that 'We simply do not know how many people are frustrated in their lives by inability ever to express themselves adequately' (para. 49). The problem is in fact a much more fundamental one, for *everyone* is frustrated at some time or another in his efforts to communicate subjective emotion. The crux of the problem is that, while words enable a child to label and to some extent discriminate his emotional responses to different situations, and thus to compare his feelings with those of other people (see pp. 56–8 above) the fact remains that the labels he uses are arbitrary signs which he is com-pelled to use for want of anything better and, although they facilitate communication up to a point, they are never flexible nor accommodating enough to symbolize precisely every feel-ing he wishes to articulate. Some feelings will always remain outside the verbally-labelled parts of the child's system, there being no symbols which can be used as convenient word-handles for them (Kelly, 1963, p. 110).

The words conventionally used to label emotions ('affec-tion', 'anger', 'anxiety', 'awe', and so forth) cannot give direct,

L

unequivocal representations of experiential events as these present themselves to different individuals. Each of these words is too general and too 'public' in character to represent adequately the detailed complexity of each individual's private experience. In his book, *The Language of Emotion* (1969), Davitz set out to compile a dictionary of emotional terms by drawing together 'commonalities of meaning' and by identifying 'areas of intersubjective agreement' on the words most commonly used to label emotion. He was forced to concede finally that the definitions arrived at were far from satisfactory, for too many of them overlapped to be truly definitive:

> 'To use a somewhat awkward quantitative metaphor, systematic knowledge in this area before the present study might be said to have been at about 5% of some theoretical potential. This research probably raises that level to something closer to 6%, and perhaps we shall never move much beyond 30 or 40%' (p. 91).

Unfortunately, an emotional label *never* gives the defining quality of that particular emotion. For example, as Kaufman (1966, p. 192) points out, the word 'love' can cover feelings ranging from motherly love, brotherly love or selfless love, to sexual love. One has only to consider the variety of contexts in which the question 'Do you love her?' might be put, to realize how ambiguous the word 'love' is. And yet, even if we had more words for 'love', in the way that Eskimo has seven words for 'snow', it is doubtful whether this would resolve the difficulty, for people might still take each word to signify something different. We must accept therefore that the words used to describe emotions are, in the final analysis, only crude, abstract symbols for attempting to pin down elusive, highly individualized subjective states, and that they seldom reflect adequately a person's innermost feelings.

This is not to say that each person is so enclosed in the world of his private subjectivity that no one else can ever hope to make reasonable inferences from the words he uses as to what he is feeling. Human beings are, after all, pretty much alike in their essential characteristics, and basically their feelings and emotions are not all that dissimilar. Nor is it to imply that words can *never* express emotion, and never arouse emotion in other people. The very choice of words one uses is indicative of one's attitudes and feelings and, as we know from experience, words have strange power to hurt, to excite, to please and to move us to tears. (I hope to say more in a subsequent book, incidentally, about the effects of the written word on a reader's emotions.)

Yet words by themselves are not a very satisfactory medium for expressing emotion. Apart from the fact that they only approximate to the emotions they attempt to describe, they are mediated by specialized areas of the higher nervous system which permit of a high degree of conscious control, so that they can be used, if necessary, to conceal or disguise emotion. There may be a social convention, for instance, that certain emotions like anger shall not be publicly expressed. Hence, it is often difficult for the teacher to penetrate to the emotion underlying a child's writing; it is much easier to detect emotion when the child is actually speaking, since speech is accompanied by latent, non-verbal messages which he may not intend to convey or not be aware of. However carefully he chooses his words he finds it difficult to control this 'silent language' of non-verbal communication, which is governed by lower, more primitive levels of his autonomic nervous system. In conversation he may be careful to use the word 'negro' rather than 'nigger' and yet involuntarily say the word 'negro' in such a way that 'nigger' is clearly implied (Argyle, 1969, p. 70).

Generally speaking, therefore, the teacher will learn more about his pupils' emotions in oral teaching situations than from their written work, for the spoken word, reinforced as it is by the speaker's eyes, facial expression and postural set, is always stronger and more personal in its impact. Written speech, as Nancy Martin points out in *Assessing Compositions* (1965), has to convey by structure, word-order, vocabulary and stylistic devices all that, in speech, is conveyed by intonation, emphasis, pauses and tempo. Written speech forces a pause between emotion and expression, so allowing more time for emotion to be brought into touch with conscience, past experience and the basic belief system. The words which we let slip in anger or annoyance we would hesitate to set down on paper (although, conversely, it may be easier to write tender feelings than to say them). Vocal expressions tend to be more immediate and less reflective than written expressions of emotion. The very effort of writing helps to dissipate the urgency of feeling.

There *are* modes of written expression which closely resemble speaking – diary entries and personal letters are obvious examples. We say that a good letter reads as though the writer were actually speaking to us, that we can almost feel the emotion behind the written symbols, behind the underlinings and the profuse exclamation marks. The 'Bam!', 'Pow!', 'Zapp!' style of the American-type comic employs all these techniques in crude, highly exaggerated form. Some teachers even try to elicit livelier writing from their pupils by contriving situations in the classroom where so-called 'honest', intense emotions can be generated. Margaret Langdon (1961), for instance, claims that by her 'intensive writing' methods children write more vividly, 'as if the emotion itself supplied the right word almost without thought'. She implies that children's writing improves in quality if written out of strongly aroused emotion. Her method is to say, for example: 'Look! There's a spider on the wall, a huge one. Quick – write down the first thing which comes into your head about it. . . . Make it brief and snappy – don't stop to think – just write what *you* feel' (p. 9).

Children are thus exhorted 'to let themselves go more', 'to put more feeling into their writing'. One wonders what kind of emotion the teacher who makes this sort of demand really expects. Presumably she does not expect children to experience the pangs which a Swinburne or a Nietzsche claim to have felt while in the throes of composition. According to

Nietzsche, 'There is the feeling that one is entirely out of hand, with the most distinct consciousness of an infinitude of shuddering thrills that pass through one from head to foot'. Nietzsche and Swinburne talked a great deal about emotion without perhaps having any very clear idea of what it is. As Gertrude Stein shrewdly observed, 'Swinburne wrote all his life about passion but you can read all of him and you will not know what passion he had.' Byron is another writer popularly associated with romantic emotion, yet, as he remarked to someone who expected him always to be at a white heat of poetic creation, 'How is a fellow to shave if he is in continual paroxysms?' In fact, it may be doubted whether aroused emotion is not too immediate and too unsettling for good writing. Where children are encouraged to 'put more feeling' into their writing the results are sometimes frankly embarrassing – as the following illustration reveals.

For the purposes of an inquiry indirectly related to the present topic I once arranged for the same piece of written material to be presented to classes of ten-, twelve-, fourteen- and seventeen-year olds. A standardized procedure for administering the test stipulated that the pupils be given the passage without advice or explanation, be allowed time to read it through twice to themselves and then, the passage having been removed, asked to write out the story in their own words. Here is the original passage, in composing which I deliberately worked for a certain austerity, flatness and spareness of language.

'Whenever possible I walk to and from work through Wollaton Park. Part of my walk lies beside a lake on which two swans, a male and a female, have lived for the past two years. Twice recently, as I walked through the park, I watched the actions of these swans.
Last Wednesday morning when I passed that way, I saw a male and a female swan resting on the shore of the lake, also another male swan swimming towards them. I had never seen three swans in the park before, and I could not

tell which of the males was the newcomer. As the swan in the water neared the others, the female rose, came down from the bank and swam towards the approaching male. For a few moments these two swam there, each rubbing the other's neck from time to time with its bill. After this, the male continued swimming towards the shore. It mounted the bank and made an attack on the other male, which in the end flew away to another part of the lake.

That same evening I saw the three swans again. As I drew near, the two males were fighting. Suddenly one of them turned aside, took off from the water, and flew away right out of the park. As it departed, the remaining swans, a male and a female, swam on the lake, occasionally dipping their heads into the water. Since then there have been only two swans in the park.'

The tendency for the majority of the pupils in my sample, from junior school children to science sixth formers, was, as I had expected, simply to recapitulate the story, omitting details here and there and adding little to it. Only a group of arts sixth formers departed from this general tendency and, to my surprise, went in for elaborate embellishment and highly self-conscious story-telling. This is how one of them re-created the anecdote:

'It was very early in the morning and, as usual, I began my daily walk to work across the fields when I came upon the unusual site of three swans on the lake.

The sun had just risen, tinting everything a brilliant red. The water appeared to be glowing with fire and the once white swans were tinged a flaming pink. The air was biting and the grass was wet with the dew. The birds were already flying in the sky, singing, with the skylark taking the lead and the various water birds, including the swans, joining in with the chorus.

As I have already mentioned, the site of three swans was very unusual because for the past two years there have only been two on the lake – one male and one female. As

I was watching, the two male swans engaged in combat, the result being that the second swan flew to another part of the lake.

After having worked that day I made a call and eventually began my return journey. The sun was now beginning to set, the air was cool, but it was a pleasant coolness. The world was silent, the birds tucked safely away in their nests. Then suddenly, as I was passing the same lake, piercing cries filled the peaceful silence. The second swan had returned and was again fighting with the other male swan. Both were flapping their wings, their heads erect and haughty and very dignified. Ripples were sent along the once placid, picturesque lake. The battle was at its climax, the red tinge of the sun seemed to signify danger in the mortal combat. But just as quickly as it started, the fighting ceased and the intruder flew away from the lake leaving it calm and peaceful as before. I do not suppose that the intruder had heard of the saying that two is company, three's a crowd.'

This piece was not untypical of the sixth arts group's response to the test. Why were their responses so different from the rest? It might be supposed that, being *arts* sixth formers, they felt that something more literary and imaginative was expected of them, or that their number included a high proportion of what Liam Hudson (1966) would call 'divergers' rather than 'convergers'. In fact, a much simpler explanation came to light. Upon investigation it transpired that the teacher presenting the test to these particular pupils had disregarded the agreed procedure and, instead of asking them simply to tell the story in their own words, she had on her own initiative exhorted them to 'put plenty of feeling and imagination into it' – with the kind of result illustrated above. The purpose of the original experiment was thus nullified and yet, quite by accident, something of interest emerged from it.

English specialists would probably agree that, for all its fluency, the above piece of writing is unconvincing and strained. The detail is cliché-ridden, ornamental and occasionally inaccurate (as when the swans are made to join in the dawn chorus!), while the trite ending suggests that the writer has not really become involved in his subject. But why should he have become personally involved in it? Nothing had happened to engage his emotions at any deep level. He had simply done his best artificially to inject 'some feeling and imagination' into his writing, rather like trying to start a cold engine without any choke. GCE-type essays on subjects designed (hopefully) to elicit emotion often produce similar insincerity and lack of personal involvement. Here is an example of such an essay, taken from the discussion pamphlet *Assessing Compositions* (1965), in which representatives of the London Association for the Teaching of English sharply expose the weaknesses in such writing. Moira, a fifteen-year old girl, is writing on the essay-title 'Alone':

> 'To me, 'alone' is a word with a very sad meaning. A person may be alone in several different ways; he may be alone literally, perhaps on a desert island or in a deserted street at night, or in any other place where no-one else is present. He may wish to be alone or have no other alternative, but he may be with a great number of other people and yet still feel alone in the world.
>
> Those for whom I have the most sympathy are orphans, as they have no family to care for them and must feel extremely alone at times. Others who I have sympathy for are those whose homes have broken up, they also must feel lonely when separated from the rest of their family.
>
> Although 'alone' has a sad meaning to some people, it has a peaceful meaning to others. Many people like to go alone for their holiday to get away from the laborious routine of work, so that they can have some peace. Others enjoy working alone as they find concentration easier. But I, personally, prefer anothers company as when you are with another person you have someone with whom you can share your interests and with whom you may confer when

seeking advice. I like to share my leisure with others but when it comes to work, I prefer to be alone.

Those who find solitude the most boring and unhappy are people like convicts who live alone as a punishment. In their case I do not have any sympathy, as their loneliness is caused by their own stupidity. If they had not broken the law, they would never have found themselves in that situation. However, there must a few people in the prison cells today who are suffering unfair sentences of imprisonment, due to being wrongly convicted of crimes which they have not committed, but only the prisoners themselves know whether this is true.

The loneliest years of one's life are the last years. Old people often live alone and find life very tedious. It is because of this that younger people should visit old people more often and help them to enjoy the last years of their life. These people feel the hardships of loneliness more than the younger people and therefore appreciate the company of others.'

This is the sort of 'top of the head' writing we can expect from children when their interest is not fully engaged, and they are reduced to spinning what they can out of a few ill-concocted paragraph headings.

So much for insincere, 'dishonest' writing. How then is genuine emotion communicated in writing? In the case of primary school children it is nearly always difficult to detect. Left to himself, the junior school child tends to write in a matter-of-fact, concrete, narrative style, with a minimum of description or conscious self-awareness. Only if you ask him to read his work aloud will it come to life, and then you may be surprised by how exciting he makes it sound. Without this extra-verbal reinforcement however, the emotion is usually hard to discern. This is the young child's natural mode of writing and to press him for expressions of emotion for which he is not ready is to invite insincerity and posturing. Wordsworth's poem *Anecdote for Fathers* is pertinent here, as a warning to those who press too hard for premature verbalizations of emotion. Significantly, this poem, which deals with the error of trying to draw from children emotions which they are too young to experience, is sub-titled (I translate): 'Don't force me, for I shall lie if you use compulsion'.

It is perhaps worth mentioning at this point that, for David Holbrook at least, there is no great difficulty in identifying emotion in children's writing, since much of this writing, he alleges, expresses psychic problems left over from infancy. In his book *Children's Writing* (1967) he presents samples of children's work as 'exercises' in interpretation for student teachers, and provides examples of his own critical comments for guidance. Exercise 2 contains the following poem written by a spastic boy:

> I fear not death alone
> But fire
> Fire burns ragingly
> My nerves are uncontrollable
> When I think of it.

Holbrook (p. 181) comments on this poem as follows: '[The writer] seems equally to fear that the fire within, of aggressiveness and hate ("ragingly") threatens his identity: or, to put it another way, he perhaps feels that the badness of hate in him has somehow caused his condition ("uncontrollable"), so that he is guilty about being spastic. The threat of annihilation seems worse than death ("I fear not death alone").' No reasons are given to support these remarkable assertions and it transpires (in an article in the March 1968 number of *Where*, in which the same interpretation re-appears) that their author has never met the child who wrote the poem. Yet in the same article he urges upon us the necessity of getting to know the child's 'true inner self', a task which, it is emphasized, requires a 'deep and sympathetic understanding'.

The first exercise in the book includes pieces of writing

by some eleven-year old children, who had been asked by a
student to write on the subject of 'apples'. I should like to
quote the first two of these pieces, with their accompanying
interpretative gloss, as a further illustration of the method
which Holbrook advises students to follow:

(A)

### Old Apples
The skins of old apples tend to be wrinkled, like an old
woman's skin. There colour is often a dull red, which however hard you rub, will never shine, and there are lots of
small brown patches. They are no longer juicy and soft and
are best eaten soon.

### Young Apples
The colour of young apples is a shiny fresh green or a
rosy, polished red. Their skin is smooth and they are the
best you can buy.

### Bad Apples
They are mostly brown and squash with maggots climbing
in and out. They are covered with a white crust of mould
and are best thrown away.

(Girl)

(B)

An apple on the window sill looks so queer, you'd be
surprised how luch and juicy it is inside, but there it stands,
green one side, red the other, it stands there, an ornament.
It's been there some time but no-one has touched it, they've
been told not to. One day, when it is old, it will go rotten
and brown and will get thrown out with the rubbish.

(Boy)'

Holbrook (p. 179) comments on these passages as follows:

'In A and B the simple processes of humanisation, of
symbolic identification can be seen. The apple becomes a
symbol of the identity, and of human life in time: for it
can seem whole, beautiful and sound (young and good) or

rotten from within (old and bad) and liable to disappear, as the dead do.

Here the underlying symbolism is very complex. Perhaps the apple is a symbol of the first 'object' of our relationship, which is the mother's breast. The "apple of our eye" always has an aspect of being "forbidden fruit" because we have once feared, in our earliest infant rages, that we shall eat the breast all up, and so consume the mother-object, and with her, ourselves. Thus the desire for an apple always contains a modicum of guilt: as a symbol the apple is very complex, and focuses many dealings with one's inner world. So, stolen apples are like gratuitous invasions of the mother's fecund body.... The joy of apples is always accompanied by the threat of wasps ("Apples evil?"), or rotten apples: the story of Man's first disobedience symbolises these fears of the consequences of "eating the object". With children, too, sex is confused with eating, and the history of thought shows how men have always found investigation, the thirst for knowledge, and the acquiring of sexual knowledge, to be dangerous and forbidden. The Fall of Adam is thus linked, unconsciously and mythologically, to the Fall of Icarus.'

This is, to say the least, a complex and highly subjective interpretation. The author appears to admit as much himself when, in connection with another child's work, he writes: '. . . who would, at first glance, see [the poem] as a clue to such an inward quest? . . . Isn't one making too much of it all? – the symbolism, love and hate, and so forth? Can one really base such generalizations on a few idly scrawled words?' (p. 8). However, these sensible misgivings are soon brushed aside. The student teacher is assured that there is a similarity between his work and that of the child psycho-analyst and that, provided this is recognized, an 'agreed consensus of opinion' on any piece of writing is sure to emerge in the end. It is emphasized however that the interpretation of children's writing is more exacting than normal literary criticism, and that it requires a special kind of training (the nature of which is unfortunately not specified).

The dangers inherent in inviting untrained students to indulge in such arbitrary, psychoanalytical symbol-hunting scarcely need pointing out. It is obvious surely that the examples of children's writing quoted above could be discussed on a very different, more literal level. For example, we are told nothing about how the student teacher introduced this topic to her eleven-year old pupils, and yet, since all five children whose work is quoted deal in turn with old apples, young apples and bad apples, it appears more than likely that the content of their writing was determined as much by the teacher's influence as by any individual 'psychic problems' which they had brought with them to the lesson. Holbrook has not really succeeded in fact in demonstrating convincingly the presence of emotion in these passages.

A more fruitful discussion of emotion in children's writing is contained in the pamphlet *Assessing Compositions*, from which Jonathan's, Howard's and Moira's essays (quoted above) are all taken. I should like now to quote another essay from this collection, one which is in certain respects analogous to Jonathan's, the essay we have already looked at in some detail.

### 'My First Dance

"Ah well I'm here now, I might as well go through with It. Right my entrance money in this pocket, some money to buy some drings in this pocket.

"Entrance money, please" said A man from behind a partition who was collecting everybody elses money. I took the money out of my pocket and slid it under the glass partition, as if I'd done it a hundred times before, and was just about to walk away when

"Here you've forgotten you change and your ticket"

I felt A deep red glow on my face as I walked back to the desk and took my sixpence and the ticket thanked him and walked away.

I was now in a small room about ten by six, It had a large opening which led to a part of what looked like a large room, where I saw only a few tables through the opening that can't be the dance floor.

"Do you want me to put you coat away?"

I said yes please and walked over to a man behind a counter "threepence, please?"

I gave him the threepence and I saw him put my coat on a long rack full of coats then beside them were three more rack also full of coats. There must be at least a hundred people here, I must know somebody.

I walked through the opening and found myself in a long rectangular room in which were many small round tables around which boys and girls sat drinking various types of drink. At the upper end of the room was a bar around which sat more boys and girls drinking and talking. I walked dorn to the other end with the intention of having a Pepsi-cola, when I got down the the bar I saw a large opening through which was the dance hall.

I stepped inside, what a large dark place, packed with more boys and girls talking, dancing and smoking. It was so dark I could hardly see, I didn't know how the people knew who their dancing with. I walked in a little bit father and began to mingle with the crowd. So many people I've never seen so many people before in my life. Along each side of the wall were small tables and chairs with small lamps which emitted a red glow. I began to look at the people dancing all the boys were wearing boots with chisel toes and trousers with no turn ups. I looked down at my feet and noticed that my trousers had turnups. No one will notice I tried to convince myself, oh good theres another boy over there with turnups on his trousers, I thought.

Whose that with his back turned towards me I'm sure I know him, It's old Robert from School Ill go over and say hello

"Hello"

"Oh Hello, What brings you here"

"Oh I had nowhere else to go" which I knew was a lie. This is the first dance I'd ever been to, I hope he wouldn't see through my lie.

"Oh by the way Pete this is Dave"

"Hi Pete"

"Hi Dave"

I felt sure I was going to have a good time Now.

MICHAEL'

Here are the panel's comments on this essay:

'In spite of the mass of detailed description this piece does not satisfy; no strong feeling is conveyed by the writer. The central feeling of loneliness demanded by the subject is again and again overlaid by assertions of self-assurance which are unconvincing. Although the narrator is thereby enabled to recover from thoughts of loneliness and of being the odd man out, he is also prevented from getting down into the experience of loneliness to express it in authentic terms of feeling. There are details of observation which ring sharply true to actual personal experience, e.g., the coat rack calculation and the trouser turn-ups, but the story lacks a focus on the central feeling and the coherence that would dictate variety of treatment of the incidents. Here all the details are given the same prominence. The story is also marred by many errors including elementary errors in punctuation' (p. 50).

As literary critical evaluation these comments are perceptive and fair. What is said about the story-telling qualities, the descriptions, the details of observation, the lack of coherence, the uniformity of treatment and the punctuation are what we would expect of an assessment which considered this piece of writing purely as English composition. It is only when comment turns upon the question of the boy's feelings that problems arise. 'No strong feeling is conveyed by the writer' ... the feeling demanded by the subject is 'overlaid by assertions of self-assurance which are unconvincing' ... the experience is not expressed in 'authentic terms of feeling'.

If however we compare Michael's essay with Jonathan's (see pp. 12–14 above) we are struck by the fact that the feelings *hinted at* in both are not basically dissimilar: in each case there is the writer's uncertainty in a novel situation, a desire not to appear odd, a wish to affiliate, some pretended sophistication. In each case self-esteem is threatened. Unfortunately, we do not know whether either essay describes a real or an imagined experience (for we certainly cannot infer this from the written evidence alone), nor do we know how much the teacher's influence may have structured each piece of writing, and without such knowledge our comments must be tentative. If, for argument's sake, we assume that both essays deal with authentic recollected experience, then what has verbalizing it achieved for each writer? Jonathan is clearly more adept at describing and differentiating his feelings: he communicates them more successfully to the reader and so tells a better story. All sorts of interesting questions now arise. Did he feel emotion more, or less, intensely than Michael while he was actually in the dance hall? Was the emotion under better control at the time because he was able to verbalize it more effectively, or was he in fact more vulnerable to emotion? What would the effect be now on both boys after writing about the dance-hall experience to repeat it (so far as any experience is repeatable)?

It is difficult to answer any of these questions satisfactorily. Previously, I argued that youngsters bring their feelings under better control once they can verbalize them, and that aroused emotion tends to be extinguished when situations are repeated and as children develop better resources for dealing with them. It would follow from this that the more integrated a person is – the more able he is to structure his experience linguistically and to cope with different situations – the less arousal he is likely to experience. The argument becomes complicated however once other functions of language enter into the matter. If (along the lines of Bernstein's hypothesis) Jonathan responds to a wider range of perceptual stimuli than Michael, by virtue of his more elaborated linguistic capacity, then presumably he is also more vulnerable to emotion. We are faced with the paradox therefore that language is both a means by which we can control our emotions and yet that the more language we internalize, the more susceptible we become to an ever-widening range of cues capable of eliciting emotion. This problem is too complex, I think, to pursue any further at the present time. (It is another issue to which I propose to return on a subsequent occasion.) Meanwhile, I shall follow the example of the Scots minister who remarked to his congregation: 'Now here we come across a very deeficult problem, my friends, and having looked it bowldly in the face, we will pass on.'

There are other problems no less difficult in identifying the emotion behind the written word which, for the present, I can do no more than mention. In the first place, children, like adults, will avoid discussing or even acknowledging certain emotions which in fact they feel very strongly. Hence, work which they write merely as exercises in class will seldom reflect their deepest emotional concerns, unless they have an especially intimate and trusting relationship with their teacher. Then, as I pointed out in Chapter 5, there are difficulties caused by the gap between adult and childhood experience. Immature attitudes to experience may seem sentimental or unreal to the adult, and yet be perfectly natural to the child. The very words that a child uses to describe his emotions moreover may carry quite different meanings and connotations for the teacher from those which they carry for the child. Another complication is that all children learn to write by imitation, so that their expressions of emotion may be 'borrowed' from another person's style of writing. This does not make their writing any the less sincere, but it does complicate the task of identifying 'felt' emotion in their writing.

M

Then, again, there are all the implications of Bernstein's findings concerning the social determinants of emotional expression. These oblige us to adjust our expectations as to the quality and range of verbalization which is attainable by children from different social classes. Finally, there is the more fundamental problem (to which Whorf, Sapir and Susanne Langer have in their different ways all drawn attention) that the very structure of language itself limits the extent to which words can ever reflect emotional experience without distorting or falsifying it.

There is not space here to enlarge on these problems but, before concluding this chapter, I should like to add a final comment on this matter of emotion in children's writing in the light of the distinction made earlier between 'aroused emotion' and 'emotional attitudes' or 'latent emotion' (see pp. 65–6 above). 'Honest' personal writing, it seems to me, is likeliest to occur whenever a child writes on subjects which concern him deeply, and which engage his real interests and strongest emotional attitudes and sentiments. It is not born of unreflecting frisson nor the yoking together of far-fetched sensational association. It contains much stronger motivational and cognitive elements than many of the 'intensive' practitioners allow, since, for the intention to be realized (I am old-fashioned enough to believe that there should always be an intention in writing) words have to be selected and carefully disposed so as to achieve maximum effect. We start writing under an emotional impulse perhaps, but writing is usually a lengthy process in which emotions cannot remain at full stretch all the time. Gradually, the original emotion fades out and the writing process becomes increasingly cognitive. As Flaubert once put it: 'I have written very tender pages without love, and burning pages with no fire in my blood. I imagined, I recollected and I combined'. This sounds almost cynical. It isn't. The last sentence describes accurately what must happen during any extended piece of creative writing.

One of the most 'emotional' things I myself ever wrote was an article on (of all subjects!) mortgage interest rate, which appeared in the *Guardian* in October 1969. I had just received notice from the building society that interest rate was being increased yet again and that this time it would be necessary to extend the period of my mortgage by several years. At the time this unwelcome news aroused strong feelings in me, I remember, and purely to relieve these feelings I determined to write the article. Having decided to do so, I then had to marshal my facts, to 'recollect and combine', in order to make the argument as telling as possible. It took two or three days to complete, during which time of course the original arousal subsided. The piece originated in strong emotional arousal, in short, but it was the persistent emotional attitude or motivation (call it what you will) which sustained it. Interestingly enough, when the article was complete, there were not more than two or three phrases in it which could by any stretch of imagination be classed as overtly 'emotive'. The strength of feeling which underlay the argument could be inferred only from its forcefulness and energy, such as these were.

When a writer's emotions are engaged 'at the time' it is more likely to be some deeply felt emotional attitude which is present than aroused emotion (indeed, the latter is often merely a hindrance). No one understood this distinction more clearly than Wordsworth, and it is ironical that his own statements on the matter, in the preface to the second edition of *Lyrical Ballads,* have been so frequently misunderstood. Margaret Langdon (p. 5) says that Wordsworth's phrase 'emotion recollected in tranquillity' was her starting-point in her search for a new expressive medium, evidently not realizing that the immediacy of feeling which she advocates as a stimulus for 'honest' writing is quite the opposite of what Wordsworth intended. As he explained in the Preface, he tried to write without prompting of 'immediate external excitement', without 'confounding' his own feelings with those he described:

'... habits of meditation have, I trust, so prompted and regulated my feelings, that my descriptions of such objects as strongly excite those feelings, will be found to carry along with them a *purpose*. If this opinion be erroneous, I can have little right to the name of a Poet. For all good poetry is the spontaneous overflow of powerful feelings: and though this be true, Poems to which any value can be attached were never produced on any variety of subjects but by a man who, being possessed of more than usual organic sensibility, had also thought long and deeply. For our continued influxes of feeling are modified and directed by our thoughts, which are indeed the representatives of all our past feelings; and, as by contemplating the relation of these general representatives to each other, we discover what is really important to men, so, by the repetition and continuance of this act, our feelings will be connected with important subjects. . . .'

We do not expect every child to become a Wordsworth, or that he should want to analyse his purposes in writing in the way Wordsworth did. But, if we wish to produce 'genuine' emotion in children's writing, we are much likelier to elicit it by inviting children to write about matters involving what Wordsworth called 'sentiment', than by relying on gross, arbitrary stimuli, which at best elicit only temporary emotional arousal, and which at worst are an invitation to perform artificial exercises.

# 8 Culture, education and emotion

The biological characteristics of emotion probably do not vary much from one age or one country to another, but the kinds of stimuli which elicit emotions, and conventions as to what are considered appropriate expressions of feeling, do – the latter being culturally determined. Some emotions, like those associated with the flight-fight reaction, are necessary for survival and the mechanisms by which these function are, as it were, biologically built-in. Other emotions are partly or wholly culturally acquired. The emotions aroused for example by the projection-test pictures which R. Goldman (1964, p. 36) employed in his research into children's readiness for religion were culturally acquired emotions, not biological ones. The pictures were (1) of a man, woman and child entering a church; (2) of a girl kneeling by her bedside; (3) of a boy looking at a torn Bible. The sight of a mutilated Bible arouses strong emotions in some children, depending on the belief-system which has previously been inculcated, but to a tiny infant this spectacle would be a matter of complete indifference. Many aesthetic emotions are likewise culturally acquired.

Children learn to express their emotions by observing how other people express theirs. In England (until very recently, at least) it has usually been thought proper to aim at the controlling or inhibiting of emotional expression (the stiff upper lip or public school ideal) whereas Mediterranean peoples have traditionally placed less emphasis on the suppressing aspect of emotional control, preferring a freer, less inhibited expression of feeling. Yet within English society there have been over the centuries as many different fashions in feeling as in taste or morality. Feelings deemed appropriate by one age in regard, say, to childbirth, sexual relationships, funerals, religion, natural scenery, prostitution or insanity, have been deemed inappropriate by another age. The melodramas of one generation have become objects of amusement to the next. In 1840 half of England wept on reading Dickens' account of the death of Little Nell; in 1971 probably no one does. This does not mean that we are any less susceptible to pathos than Dickens' readers were, but only that our tear-ducts respond to different triggers – as any cinema manager knows.

Emotions do not change basically then: all that changes is the cognitive appraisal which generates emotion, and the beliefs and attitudes which influence this appraisal. Consider, for example, how attitudes to sexual relationships have altered since the time of the Victorian manual on sex with its ideal of utter continence and its quaint belief that women have no sexual feelings. Any man who believes that woman enjoy having sexual relationships deserves to be horse-whipped, said Lord Acton. Such an attitude seems strange to us today. Yet our romantic idea that falling in love is the only desirable basis for marriage, that a man should choose his partner on a basis of feeling and court her with emotional fervour, is itself regarded by other societies as a laughable and tragic aberration. Outside Western civilization it is more common for marriages to be arranged on an economic or kinship basis.

The way children feel and express their feelings is systematically patterned by their parent society, and we are only just beginning to realize how diverse these patterning systems can be. Social anthropologists have opened our eyes to the fact that there is more than one way of bringing up children and more than one type of personality-ideal worth aiming at. It is only by studying the cultural framework which lies behind child-rearing practices however that we can begin to understand, for example, why the Mundugumor child apparently experiences shame as a physical sensation in his upper arm, or why the drawings done by Balinese children exemplify such extreme stylistic differences from those done by Iatmul, Arapesh or Manus children. Margaret Mead (1946) made a study of Balinese child-rearing practices in relation to their cultural background. She observed that there was a minimum of verbal instruction in this upbringing: that children's behaviour was controlled mainly by affective intonation, by fear symbols (wildcat, witch and scorpion) and by the discouragement of bids for personal attention. The long-term consequences of these methods, Mead found, was that Balinese children seldom showed signs of guilt or remorse; they tended toward hypochondria; they lacked perseverance, attentiveness and goal-orientated behaviour. These traits contrast sharply with those developed by many English children, and prompt us to ask whether an objective study of English child-rearing practices might not throw light on some of the more common emotional characteristics displayed by our own children.

Unfortunately, little work has been done in this country on child-rearing practices as distinct from child-rearing theory, apart from that described in the Newsons' recent books on this subject. We need much more information than we have at present about parental attitudes – information, for example, on mothers' attitudes towards weaning and toilet-training; on the systems of rewards and punishments parents use; on the degree of freedom or coercion they favour; on the values they seek to instil into their children; on the character and frequency of the casual allusions they make in reference to the child's self-image; on the kinds of fears and anxieties they are prone to pass on; on the quality of their verbal relationships with their offspring, and the prominence given within these relationships to words like 'naughty', 'bad', 'dirty', 'nasty' and 'DON'T'. It is, after all, mainly by construing and complying with their parents' attitudes and values that children develop their own emotional controls. Typically, the teacher knows next to nothing about the life the pupil lives at home, and has to operate most of the time in the dark. Similarly, the parents have only the haziest notion of what their child is doing in school, and can but speculate on why he occasionally comes home tearful and morose, and says he never wants to go back to school. On the face of it, it seems absurd that there should be so little exchange of information between the home and the school – the two chief agencies normally in shaping the child's emotional life.

We need more information too about the effects which outside cultural agencies have in shaping children's attitudes – agencies like books, radio, cinema and television. It is estimated that 66 per cent of all two- to four-year olds are regular viewers of BBC *Watch With Mother* programmes, which are designed 'For the Very Young'. Among the virtues chiefly extolled in these programmes are: cleanliness, sociability, industriousness, achievement, obedience, guilt-avoidance, the desirability of being good and of being considerate for the feelings of others. What are the long-term effects of exposing infant minds to continual advocacy of these particular virtues? Again, what is the effect on emotional development of the massive exposure to mass-media values which many older children experience today? Some eleven- to fifteen-year olds, it is estimated, watch television on average for over twenty hours a week. It is to be hoped that research workers currently engaged in this field, like J. D. Halloran and his associates in the Centre for Mass Communication Research at Leicester University, may eventually provide answers to some of these questions, in addition to the valuable information they have already produced.

Every society seeks to initiate its young into its own cultural conventions, on the tacit assumption that this is necessary both for the continuance of that society and for the well-being of the individual himself. As Erikson (1965, p. 402) puts it, 'Only an identity safely anchored in the "patrimony" of a cultural indentity can produce a workable psychosocial equilibrium.' In the more static societies of the past the processes by which cultural values were assimilated and internalized operated mainly below the level of consciousness. Today we have become almost hyperconscious about the workings of these processes, and, with this heightened awareness, doubts and misgivings have arisen concerning society's actual right to impose its own, possibly narrowly conceived, patterning system upon immature minds. How can this right be squared with the fact that different societies favour demonstrably different patterning systems and diametrically opposite sets of cultural objectives? If, as some critics suggest, our English culture is an unusually parochial and insular one, one which makes life hell for some of its members by the pressures of anxiety and guilt it induces, then what sort of health does integration with it offer? Instead of liberating us and providing healthy psychic equilibrium, claims R. D. Laing (1967), English cultural conventions cripple the lives of many of our people.

Educationists have for some years now been expressing concern about the implications of this cultural predicament for the country's educational system. Recent rebellious demonstrations by the young against the education they receive have only added to the general disquiet. It is widely felt that our present educational system is too narrowly academic and rational, that it prizes intellectual distinction at the cost of neglecting feeling (see pp. 1–2 above). It is argued that the rewards it bestows upon literacy and intellectual achievement have the effect of depressing other desirable personal qualities, like loyalty, co-operation, and consideration for other people's feelings. Hence the conviction has grown that the balance needs somehow to be redressed, that something must be done to develop the child's emotions as well as his intellect. It is a set of socio-cultural rather than psychological imperatives, in short, which has stimulated the growth of interest in affective education – imperatives loosely linked to a general apprehension concerning the spread of impersonal, dehumanizing tendencies in our society, and the incidence within this society of anti-social behaviour, violence and aggression. In these circumstances it is not surprising that educationists who have written recently about affective education have tended to subordinate psychological considerations to cultural ones, or to have adopted which-ever psychological standpoint most readily coincides with their own particular cultural stance.

For example, there is the popular notion that education should aim at a 'balancing' of reason and emotion. Jeffreys' book *Personal Values in the Modern World* (1962) contains a representative statement of this type:

> 'A human being is, or ought to be, a whole organism; and what affects one part affects the rest also. It is the business of education to foster the growth of balanced, whole persons. If education is deficient on the side of feeling, it is bound to be defective on the intellectual side; the result-ing intellectual life will tend to be arid – it will, so to speak, lack body' (p. 129).

It is here assumed, on grounds not made fully explicit, that psychic health requires some sort of harmony or balance between an emotional and a cognitive half of our nature – an assumption which has underpinned much of the discussion in recent years about general studies and liberal education. (An exclusive specialization in science rather than arts is thought to develop rationality at the expense of feeling.) It represents what many of the head teachers of infant and junior schools meant probably when, on being asked by the Plowden Committee for their views on the aims of primary education, they spoke of the desirability of "all round develop-ment', 'whole personality' and 'full development of powers'. Such vague general objectives, as the Report commented, amount to little more than 'expressions of benevolent aspiration' (para, 497).

The notion that to be healthy an organism should function as a whole obviously makes sense of a limited kind, for, physiologically speaking at any rate, the organism must function as a whole. Our biological survival depends upon the preservation of homeostatic balance, and within the fluid workings of the brain and nervous system, it is almost impossible to separate cognition from affect and volition. It cannot be inferred therefore that reason and emotion are separate entities which need to be 'balanced', or that an education which neglected the emotions would automatically lead to psychic imbalance. To think of the mind as crudely divided between a cognitive and an emotional 'side' is to employ an obsolete faculty mode of thinking which few psychologists today would accept. Apart from its psychological implausibility the chief objection to the 'whole man' ideal as an educational aim is that it seldom leads to anything more fruitful than the dreary 'Two Cultures' debate, or to the somewhat desperate hope, so much in evidence in our schools, that a balance between cognition and emotion can somehow be achieved merely by time-tabling blocks of humanities subjects against the sciences (as though the education of feeling commences only when the pupil moves from the laboratory to the arts lesson). As I attempted to show in Chapter 4, science and the practical subjects are capable, potentially at least, of playing a much greater role in affective education than is generally supposed.

Once emotion and reason are regarded as mutually opposing it is tempting to suppose that feelings are wayward, unruly elements needing to be held in check by reason – an opinion shared by Plato and Locke, two of the most influential of educational theorists. Locke (1693, para. 122) held that the 'right improvement and exercise of our reason [is] the highest perfection that a man can attain to in his life', and that passions like love, anger, fear or grief, if given to free a rein, 'clog' the mind and hinder it from the pursuit of rationality. 'When the fancy is bound by passion', he remarked (1706, para. 45), 'I know no way to set the mind free'. This view, as we saw in an earlier chapter, is still shared to some extent by teachers at present in training.

From Plato's time down to the late nineteenth century, as Bantock (1967, p. 67) points out, educationists have usually aimed at the controlling or inhibiting of emotional expression.

During the present century the influence of Freud and psychoanalytical theory have done much to change opinion on this matter. We tend nowadays to think that the ability to handle one's emotions includes expression as well as inhibition. A. S. Neill, the founder of Summerhill, the well-known progressive school, is an extreme protagonist of this view. Neill (1967, p. 133) writes: '. . . to me education is primarily an affair of the emotions; not that one should try to educate the emotions; one can only make an environment in which emotions can be lived out and expressed. I have said for years that if the emotions are free the intellect will look after itself.' Neill is not alone in regarding the uninhibited expression of emotion as virtually a matter of emotional hygiene.

The notion that unwanted emotion needs to be discharged or got rid of for the sake of psychic equilibrium underlies many of the procedures currently employed in art, craft and drama lessons – subjects which, the Newsom Report suggests, 'draw powerfully on feeling and provide both an emotional release and a channel through which feelings can be constructively employed' (para.364). Books like Joan Haggerty's *Please Miss Can I Play God?* (1966), Slade's *An Introduction to Child Drama* (1958), Way's *Development through Drama* (1967) and Hodgson and Richards' *Improvisation – Discovery and Creativity in Drama* (1966) – to suggest only a representative sample – all advocate the use of drama in schools as a means of containing incipient violence and of providing therapy for children's 'neuroses'. Newsom writes as though the discharge of inhibited feelings were a necessity for many of the children with whom that Report deals:

'Some pupils will respond best to a precise and craftsman-like approach. Others, including some of the most difficult of those with whom this report is concerned, may need a more freely emotional outlet, and find, especially through painting and modelling and carving, some means of exploring feelings which have to be inhibited in everyday life, or of vividly living out again past experiences. Here they can deal imaginatively with the real, and realistically with what is imagined. There are analogies in this with some forms of dance and drama and imaginative writing. A teacher need not venture into the dangerous realms of psychiatry to recognize that for some pupils these experiences may have a therapeutic value, and for most, a strong emotional satisfaction' (para. 377).

The thesis that 'the inner life is in sound condition only if it finds outlet', and that it is the task of the school to help children to 'play out psychologically significant situations' recurs again and again in official pronouncements on the teaching of art, craft and the humanities.

This representation of the child's life as semi-neurotic and in need of regular discharge therapy derives from psychoanalytical theory. It forms the basis of much of the remedial work carried out in special schools for children who are known to be emotionally disturbed. How accurately it depicts the normal child is a question seldom, if ever, considered. I am not concerned here to challenge the basis of psychoanalytical theory, only to call in question its misapplication to the classroom. It may be that, despite the fact that many of the Freudian concepts cannot be experimentally tested, the psychoanalytical account of the child's inner life represents a brilliant insight into phenomena which are otherwise incomprehensible, and that there are no facts of the psychic life which Freudian theory does not explain much better than any alternative theory can. Psychoanalysts point proudly to the record of success with the mentally sick which psychotherapy has achieved and they maintain that the psychoanalytical hypothesis, considered as explanation rather than as a theory capable of making verifiable predictions, cannot be improved upon. However that may be, it must be emphasized, as psychoanalysts themselves have always emphasized, that therapy is a matter for trained clinicians, not teachers.

There are common-sense objections against allowing

amateurs to practise psychiatry on children. Since a professional training in psychotherapy is not normally included in College of Education or University Education Department courses, it may be doubted whether many teachers are capable of providing appropriate curative techniques for children who are genuinely ill. In any case, as Peters (1964) and Bantock (1967, ch.1) rightly insist, the ordinary school is not a mental hygiene clinic nor a place for psychotherapy: the teacher's primary funtion is to train and instruct; it is not to cure emotional maladjustment. To the extent that teaching can influence the cognitive and perceptual elements which determine emotion, it may have therapeutic value. Such preventive therapy (if such we may call it) falls legitimately within the teacher's professional province, whereas remedial treatment belongs more properly within the psychotherapist's province. Instead of blaming emotion as irrational therefore, and seeking always to release or get rid of it, teachers should value emotion for the information it provides about the pupil. It signals information about his present state of functioning, on the basis of which the teacher can decide which educative procedures, if any, are most appropriate for meeting his immediate needs.

Some educationists are concerned less with therapy than with promoting what they call 'depth and sincerity' of feeling. The criterion for evaluating emotion then becomes its 'genuineness' – a quality easier to define perhaps in terms of what it is not, than in terms of what it actually is. Exponents of this view usually start from the assumption that our present educational system and culture are 'sick' and incapable of promoting genuine feeling. The one is said to be narrowly intellectual, the other to traffic in modes of feeling which are trivial, artificial and cheap.

Our system of education and our inferior popular culture are said to mirror the worst characteristics of the parent society – especially the latter's rationalistic, impersonal and dehumanizing tendencies. Ours is held to be a society which sets a premium on a very specialized range of human activity. Rationality and a dehumanized personality are the characteristic mental attitudes it fosters – at the expense of genuine feeling (Bantock, 1963, pp. 63–5). As compared with life in the pre-industrial society modern urban life is said to be harsh and unpleasant: in the industrial town feelings become neurotic or emasculated. 'Who will assert', Dr Leavis (1962, p. 26) demands, 'that the average member of a modern society is more fully human, or more alive, than a Bushman, an Indian peasant, or a member of one of those poignantly surviving primitive peoples, with their marvellous art and skills and vital intelligence?'

The above diagnosis reflects a view of our society, its education and culture, which is widely shared today, especially among academics. This is not the place to examine in detail its accuracy, nor to question to what extent it is based upon subjective impression employed in the service of certain cherished values. As a general comment it may be observed however that the diagnosis is somewhat pessimistic and negative in character, backward-looking in its yearnings for a sentimentalized, pre-industrial primitivism, and, as Lord Annan (1966, p. 6) points out, prejudiced both in that it fails to match its analysis of the present by a similar concern to analyse the sickness of the past, and in that it refuses to see anything good in mass popular culture. Our immediate concern here is with the recommendations for the education of emotion which stem from this diagnosis. These are not very fruitful. We are presented with the curious view that genuine feeling belongs mainly to the past, and we are invited to regard our society as one populated by thousands of manipulators of 'false' feeling, whose influence it is the business of thousands of educators to counteract.

The mass culture associated with the dehumanized society is held to be a sick, soft-centred culture – one which, as Newsom puts it, blurs our apprehensions of reality by presenting false or distorted views of people, relationships and experience in general (para. 475). A main purpose of affective education, according to this view, is to wean children away from the debilitating influence of mass culture – to persuade them, in the words of the Schools Council's Paper on *Raising the School-Leaving Age* (1965), that 'the ability to discriminate between pop music which is mawkish, sentimental or boorish, and that which evokes, however crudely, genuine human feeling, represents a gain in sensitivity that is worth having' (para. 50).

Broadly speaking, two sorts of corrective are proposed for counteracting the emotional ill-effects of exposure to mass-media values. One is for teachers to put more trust in the civilizing experience of contact with great literature. The Schools Council's *Working Paper No. 3: English* (1965) suggests that –

'The literature of both past and present can illuminate the underlying pattern of human problems today. From literature the attraction of man's good qualities can be felt at its strongest: the generosity of Cordelia's "No cause, no cause", the compassion of Wilfred Owen for his dead enemy. *The impact made on our feelings by such behaviour is a lasting one;* it helps to mould our own reactions to life, and we become in the best sense more human' (para. 3). [my italics]

Another proposal, advocated by both Holbrook (1961, pp. 17–18, 44–52) and Bantock (1963, pp. 117, 210–16), is that we should revivify the old folk culture, or develop a new one like it. Such a culture could supply the 'maturity of sensibility' England needs. It would develop vitality and more positive attitudes to life, and be a means of releasing sympathy and 'spontaneous-creative fullness of being' (the phrase is D. H. Lawrence's) such as existed in pre-industrial communities. In practical terms this means placing a broad emphasis in school on participation in speech, mime, drama and craft; it entails working through the imagist, the symbolic, the dynamic of poetry rather than the logic of prose. In folk songs like *Foggy Dew*, *The Seeds of Love* and *O Waly Waly* pupils will discover for themselves a depth and a quality of 'emotional sincerity' which popular culture lacks.

A problem in administering these remedies is to persuade the patient that he does in fact need them. Not all children respond enthusiastically to *O Waly Waly;* they don't all accept the need to read improving literature – as the Schools Council's Paper on *Raising the School-Leaving Age* frankly admits:

'Nothing is more distressing than the fact that very many pupils who leave our schools at 16 (or before) have very little good to say for what they have learnt in those subjects which are concerned with the understanding of human nature and human institutions. . . .

We are not alone in facing this problem; many other countries have made much more of a concerted attack upon the problems of teaching the humanities to the whole population, and they are in much the same case as we are' (paras. 62–3).

In fact the effectiveness of the remedies and the prognoses on which they are based are rarely, if ever, tested. (Those who advocate them might be disconcerted if they were.) There is no evidence that reading 'good' literature necessarily produces a desirable permanent effect on our feelings, any more than there is that reading inferior literature has an injurious effect. It would certainly be difficult to prove that anyone was ever 'corrupted' by reading inferior literature. I am reminded here of the student who, fascinated by this problem, once advertised for someone who had been – and received no replies!

A resuscitated folk culture is held to be especially desirable for less able children, who are said to suffer most from the pernicious effects of mass culture. According to Bantock (1963, pp. 166–7) the emotional and moral development of an elite minority can be effectively catered for by a Leavisite training in literary appreciation but, for the majority, 'some more affectively based, some less consciously elaborated methods of inducing literary appreciation' are required. This

N

entails a two-tier approach to the education of emotion – one appropriate for sheep, another for goats. The form of affective education best suited to any individual child is thus determined by some adult person's estimate of his capacity for appreciating literature. The whole field of science and, by implication, vast areas of non-literary behaviour are dismissed as relatively unimportant.

I am not for one moment implying that the reading of literature does not have a special part to play in meeting children's psychological needs. It is a means whereby the child can extend his experience by living vicariously through the experience of others, can identify with unfamiliar roles, and can explore new attitudes and emotions in a relatively detached context wherein he is safely distanced from the consequences of events. It is a means – sometimes the only means – of sharing in experiences which some sensitive stranger has deemed worth recording. In reading about how events struck another person a child may perceive a reflection of his own feelings, and find that the writer has given shape, order and coherence to his own amorphous experience (Beardsworth, 1969). This helps him to clarify his own problems and to discriminate his own emotions better. However, as I indicated in Chapter 7, there are limitations on the extent to which language can communicate emotional meaning satisfactorily, and there is a limit to the amount of illumination which the act of reading a book can shed upon any individual reader's private experience.

Those who are most vociferous in advocating the study of literature as the major vehicle for promoting affective education often appear oblivious of this fact, and to be unmindful of children's basic psychological needs. Instead of inquiring into what literature actually does for children, or following up Newsom's tentative query 'Have aim and method in English teaching kept pace with what we know about young people and how they learn?' (para, 461), they seem more concerned with preserving a particular set of cultural values. Their hope appears to be that by bringing all children, including those of very limited attainments, into contact with the civilizing experience of 'great' literature, the emotions of these children will thereby be moulded and 'refined' so as to be capable of withstanding the allegedly bad effects of commercialized popular culture. Texts prescribed for the purpose are thus chosen for their literary 'quality' rather than for their psychological relevance. The cultural aspirations underlying these proposals are remarkably similar in fact to those pursued a century ago by Sidgwick Arnold and other Victorians. Sidgwick (1868, p. 130), wanted people to study English literature as a means of 'apprehending noble, subtle and profound thoughts, refined and lofty feelings'.

The cultural standpoint upon which these proposals are based is plain to see then: what is lacking is any close analysis of feeling. The suggestion that literary experience should of necessity be central in the education of emotion has at some point to be reconciled with the problems concerning the relationship between language and emotion to which I have drawn attention, and with the Schools Council's admission that many adolescents, not only in this country but also in Sweden and the USA, are becoming increasingly hostile to the diet of literature they are given in school. Clearly, many of our school-leavers do not accept that genuine emotion resides chiefly in books. Equally unacceptable is the notion that compared with our ancestors we are emotionally emasculated – a glance at human behaviour in any school playground immediately refutes it. How one would set about proving that feelings nowadays are less 'genuine' than they were in the pre-industrial society it is difficult to imagine. And finally we must at some point face up to the fact that the insular basis of our culture, narrowly academic and literary as in some respects it is, may need eventually to be broadened to support the structure of a multi-racial society. This is how the Schools Council's *Working Paper No. 13* (1967) describes our immigrants' present cultural plight: 'They possess not only different languages from our own, but they have been bred in different cultures – with different religious beliefs, possessing different child-rearing practices, sexual controls, kinship patterns, parent-child roles and group goals concerning, for example, husband and wife (para 12).' It seems highly unlikely that an intensive course in literature or English folk culture could ever play more than a secondary role in meeting the emotional needs of the children of these immigrants.

In each of the approaches to affective education which I have discussed in this chapter there is then a perceptible cultural bias. The whole man ideal tends to be employed, by Jeffreys (1962) and by Holbrook (1961), not as a psychological concept but as a criterion for evaluating the health of society at large. Similarly, as Bantock (1967, p. 15) explains, our current preoccupation with mental health and with providing therapeutic discharge of inhibited feeling appears to be very much a phenomenon of twentieth-century, post-Freudian civilization, with its concern over the incidence of neurotic anxiety among its own members. Finally, as we have just seen, the recommendation that a child's affective education be geared to his capacity for appreciating the best in English literature seems to spring as much from a desire to preserve a certain set of cultural values as from any perceptive insight into children's emotional needs.

A strong cultural bias is also discernible in other approaches to affective education which have been proposed at various times, notably in Bloom's *Taxonomy of Educational Objectives*, Volume II (1964). In a useful article entitled 'Pandora's Box: The Affective Domain of Educational Objectives' (1970) J. H. Gribble demonstrates clearly some of the cultural assumptions underlying Bloom's taxonomy. Suggestions that affective education should aim primarily at the control of aggressive behaviour, at the refinement or enrichment of feeling, or at the development of aesthetic emotion, tend likewise to be culturally orientated.

It is not denied that the significance of cultural factors in emotional development needs emphasizing, for these are bound to influence the child's emotional life, whether we like it or not. But, if we concentrate too much upon the cultural at the expense of the psychological aspects of emotional experience, there is a danger that our objectives in affective education may become woolly and imprecise, and, as Bloom puts it, 'buried in platitudes'. There is also the risk that we may be concentrating on the child's needs in the wrong order of priority. If Maslow's (1954) surmise is correct, human motives are arranged in a hierarchy which follows an evolutionary pattern, and which ranges from lower primary motives, like hunger and fear, to higher ones, like love, esteem and, finally, self-actualization. This hierarchy, Maslow suggests, refers to the order in which motives appear in the development of the individual, and he thinks it probable that a higher motive does not usually appear until the ones below it are satisfied. Maslow's surmise is no more than hypothesis admittedly, but it serves to remind us that affective education, in the broadest sense of the term, must have regard for the child's primary emotions as well as for the more sophisticated sentiments and tastes he acquires through cultural experience. As Margaret Phillips observed (see p. 74 above), if his urgent personal needs in the practical world are not first satisfied, the child's later cultural experience may become warped and distorted.

D. A. Prestcott, reporting in 1938 on the work of an American 'Committee on the Relation of Emotion to the Educative Process', emphasized the necessity of increasing our knowledge of the psychology of emotion before we attempt to make any further prescriptions about affective education:

'[The Committee] is convinced that a long period of research and experimentation must be completed before anyone should dare speak with confidence regarding the *proper* role of affective experiences in the educative process.

The initial effort must be devoted to increasing our knowledge of the psychology of the affective life and to experiments in applying our limited knowledge through educational agencies' (p. 9).

Today, over thirty years later, it is still too early to speak with full confidence regarding the proper role of affective education. Our understanding of the causes and consequences of emotion remains far from complete, and there are questions associated with the educative process for which, as yet, we have scarcely begun to find answers. The questions, for example, of whether we should mould a child's education to his biological stage of development or his chronological age (Tanner, 1961), of how to cope with the fact that at puberty a girl's physical development may be at least two years ahead of a boy's, of the implications for the emotional life of the socio-linguistic factors mentioned by Bernstein, and of the special emotional difficulties faced by immigrant children. We know a good deal more now than was known in 1938 about the causes and the consequences of maladjustment and emotional deprivation, but we still possess little exact information about the emotional development of the normal child beyond the infancy stage.

Yet in the period since the war there have undoubtedly been advances in our knowledge of the psychology of emotion, and, in different degrees, medical research workers, physiologists, analytical philosophers, phenomenologists, ethologists, anthropologists, psycholinguists and educationists have all provided fresh insights into the subject. Unfortunately, the learned journals and books in which these insights are usually recorded tend to be widely scattered and inaccessible to the general reader. In this book therefore I have attempted to bring some of them together, in the hope that they may be of interest to students, teachers and parents. The aim of the book has not been to provide a comprehensive and exhaustive account of emotion, but to draw attention to those aspects of the child's emotional life which the teacher needs to know about and which he can legitimately seek to influence. Doubtless the book poses as many questions as it answers, but, if it sheds some light on the nature of emotion and stimulates fresh discussion of what is meant by affective education, it will have succeeded in its main purpose.

The photograph of the girl in plate 1 originally appeared in *The Guardian* at the time of the Mexico Olympic Games above the caption: *'The face of victory—Colette Besson weeps with joy after beating Lillian Board to win the gold medal in the women's 400 metres'*.

The above caption does not represent adequately perhaps the complex mixture of emotions which the girl was experiencing at the time the photograph was taken, but this illustration shows how difficult it is to identify emotion accurately in the face of a stranger if one is given no clue to the situational context. In this case (as with any still photograph) the problem of identification is further increased by the fact that the normal mobility of facial expression has been arrested in mid-sequence.

# Bibliography

ANNAN, LORD (1966), *The Disintegration of an Old Culture*, Clarendon Press, Oxford.

ARGYLE, M. (1969), *Social Interaction*, Methuen, London.

ARGYLE, M., AND DEAN, J. (1965), 'Eye-contact, distance and affiliation', *Sociometry*, **28**, 289–304.

ARNOLD, M. B. (1960), *Emotion and Personality*, 2 vols., Columbia University Press, New York.

ARNOLD, M. B. (ed.) (1968), *The Nature of Emotion*, Penguin, Harmondsworth.

ARNOLD, M. B. (ed.) (1970), *Feelings and Emotions: The Loyola Symposium*, Academic Press, New York.

ASCH, S. E. (1955), 'Opinions and Social Pressure', in S. Coopersmith (ed.), *Frontiers of Psychological Research*, Freeman, San Francisco, 1966.

ASHWELL, V. C. (1962), 'Teachers as Observers', *New Era*, **43**, 107-8.

ASSESSING COMPOSITIONS, *A Discussion Pamphlet* (1965), London Association for the Teaching of English, Blackie, London.

BANTOCK, G. H. (1963), *Education in an Industrial Society*, Faber, London.

BANTOCK, G. H. (1967), *Education, Culture and the Emotions*, Faber, London.

BAYLEY, N. (1932), 'A study of the crying of infants during mental and physical tests', *J. Genet. Psychol.*, **40**, 306-29.

BEARDSWORTH, T. (1969), 'The place of literature in moral education', *Moral Education*, **I**, 53-62.

BEATTY, W. H. (1969), 'Emotions: the missing link in education', *Theory into Practice*, **8**, 86-92.

BEDFORD, E. (1957), 'Emotions', *Aristotelian Soc. Proc.*, **57**, 281-304.

BELDOCH, M. (1964), 'Sensitivity to expression of emotional meaning in three modes of communication', in J. R. Davitz (ed.), *The Communication of Emotional Meaning*, McGraw-Hill, New York.

BERNSTEIN, B. (1958),'Some sociological determinants of perception', *Brit. J. Sociol.*, **9**, 159–74.

BERNSTEIN, B. (1959), 'A public language: some socialogical implications of a linguistic form', *Brit. J. Sociol.*, **10**, 311–23.

BERNSTEIN, B. (1960), 'Language and social class', *Brit. J. Sociol.*, **11**, 271–6.

BERNSTEIN, B. (1961), 'Social structure, language and learning', *Educl. Research*, **3**, 163–76.

BERNSTEIN, B. (1970) 'A socio-linguistic approach to socialization: with some reference to educability', in J. Gumperz and Dell Hymes (eds.), *Directions in Sociolinguistics*, Holt, Rinehart and Winston, New York.

BLOOM, B. S., *et al.* (1964), *Taxonomy of Educational Objectives. Handbook II: The Affective Domain*, Longmans, London.

BOGDONOFF, M. D., *et al.* (1961), 'The modifying effect of conforming behaviour upon limpid responses accompanying CNS arousal', *Clin. Res.*, **9**, 135.

BOWLBY, J. (1951), *Child Care and the Growth of Love*, Penguin, Harmondsworth.

BOWLBY, J. (1970), 'Attachment and loss', *Guardian*, 9 April.

BRIDGES, K. (1932), 'Emotional development in early infancy', *Child Dev.*, **3**, 324–41.

BRITTON, J. (1969), 'Talking to learn', in D. Barnes, J. Britton and H. Rosen, *Language, the Learner and the School*, Penguin, Harmondsworth.

BÜHLER, C. (1930), *The First Year of Life*, Day, New York.

CANNON, W. B. (1932), *The Wisdom of the Body*, Kegan Paul, London.

CHANCE, M. R. A. (1962), 'The interpretations of some agonistic postures: the role of "cut-off" acts and postures', *Symp. Zool. Soc., London*, **8**, 71–89.

CRUTCHFIELD, R. S. (1955), 'Conformity and character', *Amer. Psychol.*, **10**, 191–8.

CRUTCHFIELD, R. S. (1962), 'The individual in the group', in D. Krech, R. S. Crutchfield and E. L. Ballachey, *Individual in Society*, McGraw-Hill, New York.

CULLEN, M. (1967), 'Animals and communications', *The Listener*, 20 April.

DAVITZ, J. R. (ed.) (1964), *The Communication of Emotional Meaning*, McGraw-Hill, New York.

DAVITZ, J. R. (1969), *The Language of Emotion*, Academic Press, New York.

DAVITZ, J. R., AND MATTIS, S. (1964), 'The communication of emotional meaning by metaphor', in J. R. Davitz (ed.), *The Communication of Emotional Meaning*, McGraw-Hill, New York.

DIMITROVSKY, L. (1964), 'The ability to identify the emotional meaning of vocal expressions at successive age-levels', in J. R. Davitz (ed.), *The Communication of Emotional Meaning*, McGraw-Hill, New York.

DRAMA IN EDUCATION (1968), Reports on Education, Department of Education and Science, November, No. 50, HMSO.

DUFFY, E. (1941) 'An explanation of "emotional" phenomena without the use of the concept "emotion" ', *J. Gen. Psychol.*, 25, 283–93.

EKMAN, P., AND FRIESEN, W. V. (1967), 'Origin, usage and coding: the basis for five categories of non-verbal behaviour', paper at Symposium in Communication Theory, Buenos Aires, Argentina. Cited in M. Argyle, *Social Interaction*, Methuen, London.

ERIKSON, E. H. (1965), *Childhood and Society*, revised edn., Penguin, Harmondsworth.

ERIKSON, E. H. (1968), *Identity, Youth and Crisis*, Faber, London.

FELEKY, A. (1922), *Feelings and Emotions*, Proueer Press, New York.

FERNBERGER, S. W. (1928), 'False suggestion and the Piderit model', *Amer. J. Psychol.*, 40, 562–8.

FLANAGAN, J. C. (1961), 'Leadership skills: their identification, development and evaluation', in L. Petrullo and B. M. Bass (eds.), *Leadership and Interpersonal Behaviour*, Holt, Rinehart and Winston, New York.

FRAISSE, P. (1968), 'The emotions', in P. Fraisse and J. Piaget (eds.), *Experimental Psychology: its Scope and Method, V, Motivation, Emotion and Personality*, by J. Nuttin, P. Fraisse and R. Meili, trans. by Mme. A. Spillmann, Routledge, London.

FREUD, A. (1931), *Introduction to Psycho-analysis for Teachers*, Allen and Unwin, London.

FREUD, S. (1948), *Beyond the Pleasure Principle*, Hogarth Press and Institute of Psycho-Analysis, London.

FUNKENSTEIN, D. H. (1955), 'The physiology of fear and anger', in S. Coopersmith (ed.), *Frontiers of Psychological Research*, Freeman, San Francisco, 1966.

GARDNER, D. B. (1964), *Development in Early Childhood: The*

*Preschool Years*, Harper and Row, New York.

GILCHRIST, J. C., AND NESBERG, L. S. (1952), 'Need and perceptual change in need-related objects', *J. Exper. Psychol.*, **44**, 369–76.

GOLDMAN, R. J. (1964), *Religious Thinking from Childhood to Adolescence*, Routledge, London.

GOODENOUGH, F. L. (1931), *Anger in Young Children*, Minneapolis Univ. Press.

GRAY, D. (1969), 'Pancho wins the longest match', *Guardian*, 26 June.

GRIBBLE, J. H. (1970), 'Pandora's box: the affective domain of educational objectives', *J. of Curric. Studies*, **2**, 11–25.

GROSSMAN, H. (1965), *Teaching the Emotionally Disturbed*, Holt, Rinehart and Winston, New York.

HAEZRAHI, P. (1954), *The Contemplative Activity*, Allen and Unwin, London.

HAGGERTY, J. (1966), *Please Miss Can I Play God?* Methuen, London.

HALLIDAY, M. A. K. (1968), 'Language and experience', *Educl. Review*, **20**, 95–106.

HARLOW, H. F. (1959), 'Love in infant monkeys', in S. Coopersmith (ed.), *Frontiers of Psychological Research*, Freeman, San Francisco, 1966.

HARRISON, R. P. (1965), 'Pictic analysis: towards a vocabulary and syntax for the pictorial code: with research on facial communication', *Diss. Abstr.*, **26**, 519.

HEBB, D. O. (1949), *The Organization of Behaviour*, Wiley, New York.

HERON, W. (1954), 'The pathology of boredom', *Scient. Amer.*, January 1957; W. H. Bexton, W. Heron and T. H. Scott (1954), 'Effects of decreased variation in the sensory environment', *Canadian J. Psychol.*, **8**, 70–6.

HODGSON, J. AND RICHARDS, E. (1966), *Improvisation: Discovery and Creativity in Drama*, Methuen, London.

HOLBROOK, D. (1961), *English for Maturity*, Cambridge Univ. Press.

HOLBROOK, D. (1967), *Children's Writing: A Sampler for Student Teachers*, Cambridge Univ. Press.

HOLBROOK, D. (1968), 'My interpretations of children's writing', *Where*, March 1968.

HOLMES, F. B. (1936), 'An experimental investigation of a method of overcoming children's fears', *Child Develop.*, **7**, 6–30.

HOLT, J. C. (1964), *How Children Fail*, Pitman, New York.

HUDSON, L. (1966), *Contrary Imaginations*, Methuen, London.

HUGHES (1966), *Freefall to Freeway*, film made by Hughes Aircraft Company, Culver City, California.

HULL, C. L. (1951), *Essentials of Behaviour*, Yale Univ. Press, New Haven, Conn.

ISAACS, S. (1932), *The Nursery Years: the Mind of the Child from Birth to 6 Years*, Routledge, London.

JAMES, D. (ed.) (1957), *Outward Bound*, Routledge, London.

JECKER, J. D., *et al.* (1965), 'Improving accuracy in interpreting non-verbal cues of comprehension', *Psych. in the Schools*, 2, 239–44.

JEFFREYS, M. V. C. (1962), *Personal Values in the Modern World*, Penguin, Harmondsworth.

JERSILD, A. T. (1946), 'Emotional development', in L. Carmichael (ed.), *Manual of Child Psychology*, Wiley, New York.

JERSILD, A. T. (1952), *In Search of Self*, Columbia University, New York.

KAUFMAN, I. (1966), *Art and Education in Contemporary Culture*, Macmillan, New York.

KELLY, G. A. (1963), *A Theory of Personality: The Psychology of Personal Constructs*, Norton Library, New York.

KENDON, A., AND EX, J. (1965), 'A notation for facial postures and bodily position', in M. Argyle, *Social Interaction*, Methuen, London.

KENNY, A. (1963), *Action, Emotion and Will*, Routledge, London.

KLEIN, M., AND RIVIERE, J. (1937), *Love, Hate and Reparation*, Hogarth Press and Institute of Psycho-Analysis, London.

KÖHLER, W. (1927), *The Mentality of Apes*, trans. by E. Winter, Routledge, London.

KRECH, D. (1968), 'The chemistry of learning', adapted from a speech to Three National Seminars on Innovation, sponsored by the US Office of Education and the Charles F. Kettering Foundation, in Honolulu, July 1967, *Saturday Review*, January 20, 1968.

KROUT, M. H. (1954a), 'An experimental attempt to produce unconscious manual symbolic movements', *J. General Psychol.*, 51, 93–120.

KROUT, M. H. (1954b), 'An experimental attempt to determine the significance of unconscious manual symbolic movements', *J. General Psychol.*, 51, 121–52.

KRUEGER, F. (1928), 'Das Wesen der Gefühle', abridged and trans.

by M. B. Arnold, in M. B. Arnold (ed.) *The Nature of Emotion*, Penguin, Harmondsworth.

LAING, R. D. (1967), *The Politics of Experience and The Bird of Paradise*, Penguin, Harmondsworth.

LANGDON, M. (1961), *Let the Children Write*, Longmans, London.

LANGER, S. K. (1953), *Feeling and Form*, Routledge, London.

LANGER, S. K. (1967), *Mind: An Essay on Human Feeling*, vol. I., John Hopkins Press, Baltimore.

LAWRENCE, D. H., 'To women, as far as I'm concerned', in V. de S. Pinto and W. Roberts (eds.) *The Complete Poems of D. H. Lawrence*, 2 vols., Heinemann, London, (1964).

LAZARUS, R. S. (1966) *Psychological Stress and the Coping Process*, McGraw-Hill, New York.

LAZARUS, R. S., *et al.* (1970), 'Towards a cognitive theory of emotion', in M. B. Arnold (ed.), *Feelings and Emotions: The Loyola Symposium*, Academic Press, New York.

LEAVIS, F. R. (1962), *Two Cultures: The Significance of C. P. Snow*, Chatto and Windus, London.

LEEPER, R. W. (1948), 'A motivational theory of emotion to replace "emotion as disorganized response" ', *Psychol. Rev.*, **55**, 5–21.

LEEPER, R. W. (1970), 'The motivational and perceptual properties of emotions as indicating their fundamental character and role', in M. B. Arnold (ed.), *Feelings and Emotions: The Loyola Symposium*, Academic Press, New York.

LENROW, P. B. (1965), 'Studies of sympathy', in S. S. Tomkins and C. E. Izard (eds.), *Affect, Cognition and Personality*, Springer, New York.

LEVY, P. K. (1964), 'The ability to express and perceive vocal communications of feeling', in J. R. Davitz (ed.), *The Communication of Emotional Meaning*, McGraw-Hill, New York.

LEWIS, M. M. (1963), *Language, Thought, and Personality, in Infancy and Childhood*, Harrap, London.

LINDSLEY, D. B. (1950), 'Emotions and the electroencephalogram', in M. R. Reymert (ed.), *Feelings and Emotions: The Mooseheart Symposium*, McGraw-Hill, New York.

LINDSLEY, D. B. (1951), 'Emotion', in S. S. Stevens (ed.), *Handbook of Experimental Psychology*, Wiley, New York.

LOCKE, J. (1693), *Some Thoughts Concerning Education*, (ed.), R. H. Quick, Cambridge Univ. Press, 1934.

LOCKE, J. (1706), *Of the Conduct of the Understanding*, in J. W.

Adamson (ed.), *The Educational Writings of John Locke*, Cambridge Univ. Press, 1912.

LOUKES, H. (1965), *New Ground in Christian Education*, SCM Press, London.

LURIA, A. R. (1961), *The Role of Speech in the Regulation of Normal and Abnormal Behaviour*, Pergamon, London.

LURIA, A. R. AND YUDOVITCH, F. I. (1959), *Speech and the Development of Mental Processes in the Child*, (ed.), J. Simon, Staples Press, London.

MACKENZIE, R. F. (1965), *Escape from the Classroom*, Collins, London.

MANDLER, G. (1962), 'Emotion', in R. Brown, E. Galanter, E. Hess and G. Mandler (eds.), *New Directions in Psychology*, Holt, Rinehart and Winston, New York.

MARTIN, I. (1965), 'Emotion as behaviour', *New Society*, 16 December: No. 5 in symposium 'Anatomy of the Emotions'.

MASLOW, A. H. (1954), *Motivation and Personality*, Harper and Row, New York.

MASSERMAN, J. H. (1948), 'A biodynamic psychoanalytic approach to the problems of feeling and emotion', in M. L. Reymert (ed.), *Feelings and Emotions: The Mooseheart Symposium*, McGraw-Hill, New York.

MCCLELLAND, D. C. (1955), *Studies in Motivation*, Appleton Century Crofts, New York.

MCDOUGALL, W. (1908), *An Introduction to Social Psychology*, Methuen, London.

MEAD, M. (1928), *Coming of Age in Samoa*, Penguin, Harmondsworth.

MEAD, M. (1946), 'Research on primitive children', in L. Carmichael (ed.), *Manual of Child Psychology*, Wiley, New York.

MEHRABIAN, A. (1968), 'The inference of attitudes from the posture, orientation, and distance of a communication', *J. Consult. Psychol.*, **32**, 296–308.

MOLLER, L. (1968), 'The farmyard and us', *Guardian*, 14 February.

MORRIS, D. (1967), *The Naked Ape*, Cape, London.

MORRISON, A., AND MCINTYRE, D. (1969), *Teachers and Teaching*, Penguin, Harmondsworth.

MURRAY, E. J. (1964), *Motivation and Emotion*, Prentice-Hall, New Jersey.

MURRAY, H. A. (1943), *Thematic Apperception Test Manual*, Harvard University Press, Cambridge, Mass.

NEILL, A. S. (1962), *Summerhill: A Radical Approach to Education*, Gollancz, London.

NEILL, A. S. (1967), *Talking of Summerhill*, Gollancz, London.

NEILSEN, G. (1962), *Studies in Self Confrontation*, Munksgaard, Copenhagen.

NEWSOM REPORT (1963), *Half Our Future:* A Report of the Central Advisory Council for Education (England), HMSO.

NEWSON, L. J. AND E. A. (1963), *Infant Care in an Urban Community*, Allen and Unwin, London.

NEWSON, L. J. AND E. A. (1966), *Patterns of Infant Care in an Urban Community*, Penguin, Harmondsworth.

NEWSON, L. J. AND E. A. (1968), *Four Years Old in an Urban Community*, Allen and Unwin, London.

NIBLETT, W. R. (1963), *Moral Education in a Changing Society*, Faber, London.

OESER, O. A. (1955), *Teacher, Pupil, and Task*, Tavistock Publications, London.

OLDS, J. (1956), 'Pleasure centres in the brain', in S. Coopersmith (ed.), *Frontiers of Psychological Research*, Freeman, San Francisco.

OPIE, I. AND P. (1969), *Children's Games in Street and Playground*, Oxford Univ. Press.

OSGOOD, C. E. (1967), 'Radical sentences', *The Listener*, 19 October.

OSGOOD, C. E., *et al.* (1957), *The Measurement of Meaning*, Univ. of Illinois Press, Urbana.

PAYNE, D. A., AND FARQUHAR, W. W. (1962), 'The dimensions of an objective measure of academic self-concept', *J. Educ. Psychol.*, **53**, 187–92.

PECK, R. F., AND HAVIGHURST, R. J. (1960), *The Psychology of Character Development*, Wiley, New York.

PERKINS, H. V. (1958), 'Factors influencing change in children's self-concepts', *Child Dev.*, **29**, 221–30.

PETERS, R. S. (1964), ' "Mental health" as an educational aim', in T. H. B. Hollins (ed.), *Aims in Education*, Manchester Univ. Press.

PETERS, R. S. (1966), *Ethics and Education*, Allen and Unwin, London.

PETERS, R. S., AND MACE, C. A. (1962), 'Emotions and the category of passivity', *Aristotelian Soc. Proc.*, **62**, 117–42.

PHILLIPS, M. (1937), *The Education of the Emotions*, Allen and

Unwin, London.

PIAGET, J. (1953), 'Art education and child psychology', in E. Ziegfield (ed.), *Education and Art*, UNESCO, Paris.

PLOWDEN REPORT (1967), *Children and their Primary Schools:* A Report of the Central Advisory Council for Education (England), vol. I, HMSO.

POSTMAN, L., BRUNER, J. S., AND MCGINNIES, E. (1948), 'Personal values as selective factors in perception', *J. Abn. Soc. Psychol.*, **43**.

POTTER, B. *The Tale of Two Bad Mice*, Warne, London.

PRESCOTT, D. A., (ed.) (1938), *Emotion and the Educative Process:* A Report of the Committee on the Relation of Emotion to the Educative Process, American Council on Education, Washington, DC.

*Primary Education. Suggestions for the Consideration of Teachers and Others Concerned with the Work of Primary Schools* (1959), HMSO.

QUOIST, M. (1963), *Prayers of Life*, Logos Press, Gill, Dublin.

READ, H. (1943), *Education Through Art*, Faber, London.

REYMERT, M. L., (ed.) (1950), *Feelings and Emotions: The Mooseheart Symposium*, McGraw-Hill, New York.

ROGERS, C. R. (1951), *Client-centered Therapy*, Houghton Mifflin, Boston, Mass.

ROSENTHAL, R., AND JACOBSON, L. (1968), *Pygmalion in the Classroom: Teacher Expectation and Pupils' Intellectual Development*, Holt, Rinehart and Winston, New York.

ROUSSEAU, J. J. (1762), *Emile*; see W. Boyd (ed.). *Emile for Today*, Heinemann, London (1956).

RYCROFT, C. (1968), *Anxiety and Neurosis*, Allen Lane, Penguin Press, Harmondsworth.

RYLE, G. (1949), *The Concept of Mind*, Hutchinson, London.

SCHACHTER, S., AND SINGER, J. E. (1962), 'Cognitive, social and physiological determinants of emotional state', *Psychol. Rev.*, **69**, 379–99.

SCHLOSBERG, H. (1941), 'A scale for judgment of facial expressions', *J. Exper. Psychol.*, **29**, 497–510.

SCHOOLS COUNCIL (1965), *Raising the School Leaving Age*, Working Paper No. 2, HMSO.

SCHOOLS COUNCIL (1965), *English: A Programme for Research and Development in English Teaching*, Working Paper No. 3, HMSO.

o

SCHOOLS COUNCIL (1967), *English for the Children of Immigrants*, Working Paper No. 13, HMSO.

SHERMAN,M.(1927,1928), 'The differentiation of emotional responses in infants', *J. Comp. Psychol.*, **7**, 265–84; ibid, 335–41; **8**, 385–94.

SIDGWICK, H. (1868), 'The theory of classical education', in F. W. Farrar (ed.), *Essays on a Liberal Education*, Macmillan, London.

SLADE, P. (1958), *An Introduction to Child Drama*, Univ. of London Press.

SMOCK, C. D. (1955), 'The influence of psychological stress on the "Intolerance of ambiguity" ', *J. Abn. Soc. Psychol.*, **50**, 177.

SPENS REPORT (1938), *Secondary Education with special reference to Grammar Schools and Technical High Schools:* A Report of the Consultative Committee on Secondary Education, HMSO.

SPITZ, R. A. (1963), 'Ontogenesis, the proleptic function of emotion', in P. H. Knapp (ed.), *Expression of the Emotions in Man*, International Univs. Press.

SPOCK, B. (1969), *Baby and Child Care*, Bodley Head, London.

STAINES, J. W. (1958), 'The self-picture as a factor in the classroom', *Brit. J. Educ. Psychol.*, **28**, 97–111.

STORR, A. (1968), *Human Aggression*, Allen Lane, Penguin Press, Harmondsworth.

SUTTIE, I. D. (1948), *The Origins of Love and Hate*, Kegan Paul, London.

TAGGART, P., AND GIBBONS, D. (1967), 'Motor-car driving and the heart rate', *Brit. Med. J.*, **I**, 411–2.

TANNER, J. M. (1961), *Education and Physical Growth*, Univ. of London Press.

TAVISTOCK INSTITUTE OF HUMAN RELATIONS (1969), *John, 17 months: Nine Days in a Residential Nursery*, a film by J. and J. Robertson, Concord Films Council, Ipswich.

TOLSTOY, L. (1865–69), *War and Peace*, trans. by L. and A. Maude (1959), Macmillan, London.

VALENTINE, C. M. (1962), *The Experimental Psychology of Beauty*, Methuen, London.

VAN HOOFF, J. A. R. A. M. (1967), 'The facial displays of the Catarrhine monkeys and apes', in D. Morris (ed.), *Primate Ethology*, Weidenfeld and Nicolson, London.

WARREN, H. C. (ed.) (1934), *Dictionary of Psychology*, Houghton Mifflin, Boston, Mass.

WAY, B. (1967), *Development Through Drama*, Longmans, London.

WHITE, R. W. (1959), 'Motivation reconsidered: the concept of competence', *Psychol. Rev.*, 66, 297–333.

WILSON, J., WILLIAMS, N., AND SUGARMAN, B. (1967), *Introduction to Moral Education*, Penguin, Harmondsworth.

WOLF, S., AND WOLFF, H. G. (1943), *Human Gastric Function*, Oxford Univ. Press, New York.

WOODWORTH, R. S. (1940), *Psychology*, Henry Holt, New York.

WORDSWORTH, W. (1798), 'Anecdote for fathers', in E. de. Selincourt (ed.), *Poetical Works*, Oxford, 1904.

WORDSWORTH, W. (1798), 'Preface to lyrical ballads', in E. de Selincourt (ed.), *Poetical Works*, Oxford, 1904.

YOUNG, P. T. (1961), *Motivation and Emotion*, Wiley, New York.

# Index

# Index